African American Men
from Slavery to the Here and Now

African American Men
from Slavery to the Here and Now

Charles Lucas

J. Kenkade
PUBLISHING®

Little Rock, Arkansas

African American Men from Slavery to the Here and Now
Copyright © 2020 by Charles Lucas

J. Kenkade Publishing
6104 Forbing Rd
Little Rock, AR 72209

www.jkenkadepublishing.com

J. Kenkade Publishing is a registered trademark.

Printed in the United States of America
ISBN 978-1-944486-74-7

Table of Contents

Introduction

This book is an overview of great African American Men and how they have fared as leaders from the brutality of slavery to where we are today after the election of the first African American President of the United States of America. I focused on leaders in areas such as in the educational field, the religious sector, corporate America, the United States military, and in the United States government. I chose this particular topic because as I look around, I recognize that African American men are still behind in several areas throughout America. It is the year 2020, some 155 years after the 1865 ratification of the Thirteenth Amendment of the United States Constitution. According to the U.S. Census Bureau there were approximately 4,500,000 African Americans during that time representing about 13.5% of the population of the United States. Over 400,000 were free men and over 3 million were slaves (DeShay, 2010). Today there are over 42 million African Americans in the United States, still hovering around 13% of the total population. It seems the stories of several great African American men have been left out of the books currently used in schools today. I wish to create a collection of these stories and show what impact Black men have played in shaping America into what we have today. We all have heard of greats such as George Washington Carver, Martin Luther King Jr. and our former President of the United States, Barack Obama. There are several more unheard stories of Black men who stepped into leadership roles in adverse conditions associated with the racism that developed in the United States once the African American slave was deemed property and had no rights. I wish this to be an educational source full of motiving information for future generations, a good read for the curious, and hopefully put some stereotypes about African American Men to bed.

CHAPTER I

•••

Background of African Americans up to 1865

This is a brief overview about the history of African Americans prior to the American Civil War which led to their freedom in 1865. It has been documented throughout history that most Black American origins lead back to West Africa. Eastern Africa and Angola contributed to the beginning of the slave trade by facilitating the delivery of West African captives to the new world (Darlene Clark Hine, p. 4). Based on historical facts from archeological and anthropological studies, historians have pieced together how the West African people lived prior to the Atlantic slave trade. The people of West Africa had a rich and varied history and culture long before European slavers arrived. They had a wide variety of political arrangements including kingdoms, city-states and other organizations, each with their own languages and culture. Art, learning, and technology flourished, and Africans were especially skilled in subjects like medicine, mathematics and astronomy (National Museums Liverpool, 2013). They made fine luxury items in bronze, ivory, gold and terracotta for both local use and trade. By the early sixteenth century most West Africans were farmers and typically lived in small villages within their respected kingdom (Darlene Clark Hine).

They developed a social status system within their society which was run by monarchs. The monarchs forcefully acquired power by commanding armies, taxing commerce, and accumulating wealth. They considered themselves to be royalty or divine in nature. Beneath the royalty were several different classes such as land nobles, warriors, peasants and bureaucrats. There were even lower classes such as blacksmiths, butchers, weavers, carvers, and historians (Darlene Clark Hine, p. 17).

Slavery had also been a part of their social system for thousands of years. Conflicts between monarchs produced war prisoners, which did not exclude women and children. Those war prisoners were originally used for trading in the early years of slave trade. Their slavery system had many faces. Some captives were held without rights, while children born to enslaved parents were protected from being sold away from the area in which they were born. Slaves that were royalty prior to their capture often still exercised power over lower class free people and could still own property. The slaves and peasant farmers often lived just as well as the landowners themselves. Second and third generation slave's living conditions were not much different than free Africans. In Africa, slavery functioned as a means of assimilation and was not as oppressive or brutal as slavery in America (Darlene Clark Hine, p. 17).

After Christopher Columbus discovered the Americas and the early settlers arrived, there was an attempt to enslave the American Indians. Many of the indigenous people either died of disease brought by those settlers, or they died from the harsh labor and conditions imposed on them by their captors. The lack of laborers in America turned colonialist attention to a means of more permanent labor and prompted capitalists to begin the Atlantic slave trade with Africa (Darlene Clark Hine, p. 26).

The purchasing of humans in Africa began in 1472 with Portuguese merchants. When the Portuguese first sailed down the Atlantic coast of Africa in the 1430's, they were initially only interested in one thing: gold (A&E Television Networks, LLC., 2013). The Portuguese brought in copper, cloth, tools, wine, horses, and eventually arms. In exchange, they received gold, pepper, and ivory. Over time the Portuguese began making money by simply transporting slaves up and down the coast to different trading posts which were run by the Islamic empire (National Museums Liverpool, 2013). A very small market developed for African slaves for use as domestic workers in Europe and as field workers on the sugar plantations of the Mediterranean. This market ballooned into what came to be known as the North Atlantic slave trade (National Museums Liverpool, 2013). Slaves were in abundance because of the civil unrest in Africa itself. The domestic warfare, along with village raids and kidnappings, produced over eleven million slaves between the years of 1472 and 1870 (Darlene Clark Hine, p. 30).

The slave trade was dominated by the Portuguese and the Spanish, who were equipped with vessels capable of carrying large numbers of human cargo. Most of the slaves were sold to the British North American colonies; however, the expansion of their empires into the Caribbean, Mexico, and South America also demanded laborers for their survival. Those colonies produced spices, sugar, and other small crops for their motherlands. Those crops did not compare in demand to the newly found cash crops in America such as tobacco, rice, cotton, and indigo (A&E Television Networks, LLC., 2013). The demand for those goods made the slave trade so profitable, and other countries soon turned their attention to new human trafficking market (Darlene Clark Hine, p. 29).

Historians account for Africans arriving in America as early as 1619 and living in the Jamestown colony. Unlike slavery in Africa, American slavery was based on race (Darlene Clark Hine, p. 30). Between 1620 and 1670, black and white people worked as indentured servants and were considered not free, but by the year 1700 slave owners and farmers started to develop a distinction between the two races. White servants were not as abundant as the blacks, and the labor force quickly became indentured white servants and enslaved blacks. White indentured servants eventually earned their freedom once they had worked off their debt. Most went into servitude to secure a ride to the newly found Americas. Black's option to freedom eventually was taken away because they were captives rather than volunteers. Slave labor was in demand more than ever, and between the years 1700 and 1750 there were more than 150,000 African slaves in Virginia, Maryland, Delaware and North Carolina (Darlene Clark Hine, p. 56). South Carolina and Georgia had over 40,000 slaves between them, which outnumbered the white population. During that decade, colonies revised their laws to establish that blacks could be kept in slavery permanently, generation after generation. Slavery continued to expand at a rapid pace and because of the growing numbers, and a rise in fear of a revolt, it became more brutal and oppressive for African Americans.

Once the slaves arrived at their new captive home, they were divided into work gangs according to their capabilities. There were three types of gangs. The first type consisted of the young strong men that could lift, plow, and endure long hours of field work. The second type was the women and elderly who did lighter work such as cooking, cleaning the owner's house, rearing children, and tending to the

animals. The third type was the children who carried water and food to the field gangs (Darlene Clark Hine, p. 41).

Many Africans had difficulty surviving in the new land
because most would be sick and weak with disease from
the sub-human conditions on the ships. Conditions aboard
the slave ships were wretched. Men, women, and children
were crammed into every available space and denied ade-
quate food, water, or breathing space. Malaria, smallpox,
yellow fever, and poor sanitation took the lives of several slaves during the voyage and continued to plague them
even after they reached America. The slaves that survived
were met with even more challenges in the new land.
Upon arrival, they had to adapt to the diet and the climate
in America. Language was also a barrier that the owners and the slaves alike had to overcome (Walsh, 1829).

Despite the harsh voyage and being separated from
their families and homeland, most Africans still retained vivid memories of home. The resilience of the Africans who survived the slave trade and slavery in America
was incredible. Even after the brutality changed their be-
havior, it did not take away their heritage (Darlene Clark
Hine, p. 43). The newly formed slave laws stripped African slaves in America of their legal and personal rights.
Throughout their tragic journey, African Americans established an identity and played a significant role in establishing the America we know today (Sanders, 2010, p. 9).

Prior to my research on this topic I had never heard the
mention of the arrival of twenty Africans in 1619, which
should be credited as the actual heroes of Jamestown, Virginia. The diminishing numbers of enslaved Native Indians left the settlement in distress. The lack of laborers and
knowledge of farming by the early settlers threatened their
survival. Among the small group of Africans, several were
experienced enough to grow crops and produce enough to

provide for the struggling colony and to trade. This was only the beginning of the contributions African Americans made throughout the history of America (Sanders, 2010, p. 8).

Up until the late 1700's, African Americans lived in different circumstances in White America. In the northern colonies such as Massachusetts, where the climate would not support the growth of larger cash crops, most African slaves lived in their master's home along with his family. The farms were worked by just one or two slaves and were significantly smaller than the southern plantations which required larger labor forces (Darlene Clark Hine, p. 67).

Between the years of 1700 to 1770, more than 80,000 Africans were brought to the tobacco colonies in Virginia, Maryland, Delaware, and North Carolina. Slavery began taking the form it kept for some 165 years. It was during this era of American history where the economic development of the region depended tremendously on African slave labor (Darlene Clark Hine, p. 56). A large part of America was built by the labor of these men, women, and children. The era also gave some of the Africans that arrived early the opportunity to gain an education, buy their freedom, and own businesses in some of the Northern colonies.

The New England colonies followed Puritan religious principles, and their form of slavery was less oppressive. The new attitude towards blacks caused some whites to develop laws such as the slave codes and curfews in order to minimize the chance of insurrection (Bank.WBGH, PBS Online Part 4, 2013). The law imposed harsh physical punishments since enslaved people did not own property and could not be required to pay fines. It stated that slaves needed written permission to leave their plantation, and that slaves found guilty of murder or rape would be hanged. For robbery or any other major offense, a slave would receive sixty lashes and be placed in the stocks, where his or her ears would be cut off. For minor offenses, such as associating with Whites; slaves would be whipped, branded, or maimed (Bank.WBGH, 2013).

Many slaves began to rebel and escape from the southern plantations and seek freedom in New England. These actions lead to the passing of the Fugitive Slave Act in 1793, which stated that fugitive or escaped slaves could be returned to their masters. Prior to that, free Blacks and escapees prospered in the slave free Northern States. Free African Americans also began to defend and protect the new land and prosper just as the White Americans did.

One of the first notable displays of loyalty of an African American from an escaped slave was in 1770 by a man named Crispus Attucks. Attucks was considered the first martyr of the American Revolution. He led the crowd in Boston in protest of the British occupation and was the first one gunned down by the British Soldiers. The shot heard around the world actually involved a Black man seeking the same equality and rights as the others involved in the Boston Massacre. Black men also fought bravely throughout the American Revolution. Prince Estabrook was a Black slave and Minutemen Private who fought and was wounded at the Battle of Lexington, the first battle of the American Revolutionary War (Darlene Clark Hine). An undated broadside from the time identified him as "a Negro Man", spelled his name E-a-s-t-e-r-b-r-o-o-k-s, and listed him among the wounded from Lexington. Peter Salem was a free African American who served as a Soldier in the American Revolutionary War and was actually granted his freedom as a condition for his enlistment in the Continental Army (Sanders, 2010). Peter Salem enlisted in the militia in 1775, served in Colonel James Frye's regiment, and is best remembered today for his actions during the Battle of Bunker Hill. He is credited with mortally wounding British Lieutenant Colonel James Abercrombie (Darlene Clark Hine). Many other black men not mentioned by name served in all black units such as the First Rhode Island Regiment, which fought in the Battle of Yorktown, the final conflict in the American Revolution. These brave men demonstrated that black men could be loyal citizens of America and were proud to defend its soil. Black men fought in every major battle of the Revolutionary War.

By 1790, educated elite Black men began to provide leadership in religion, economic advancement, and racial politics. This group of black men contradicted the popular American belief that blacks were not capable of being equal. Blacks continued to influence the growth of America and bravely fought in the War of 1812; however, the memories of the patriotic service of Black men in the American Revolution had long faded. Because of the White's fear of a slave revolt they hesitated to use Blacks in the War. Two regiments were formed after the British burned Washington D.C. and turned their attention towards Philadelphia and New York. The British failed to advance after being defeated in Baltimore, so the "Black Brigade" never saw action. New York offered the men freedom and their master's compensation. Black men later served in the brutal American Civil War which brought African American slavery to an end.

Prior to the Civil War there were several events that led to the freeing of the African American slaves. The first was Congress passing the Northwest Ordinance of 1787, which changed the way land was sold, created public schools, established territorial government and called for an immediate end to slavery. It limited slave owners to areas south of the Ohio River (Darlene Clark Hine, p. 101). The Ordinance and several other proposals concerning slavery were fueled by Anti-Slavery Societies. One of the most widespread was the Pennsylvania Society for Promoting the Abolition of Slavery, which was formed in 1787 and led by Benjamin Franklin. Similar societies were also formed in the states of New Jersey, Connecticut, and Virginia. From 1794 through 1832, these societies operated in accordance with the intent to improve the conditions of the African population in America (Darlene Clark Hine, p. 101).

The abolitionists worked to end the slave trade and lobbied Congress to pass the Act of 1807. The Act was meant to eliminate all American participation in the trade. Passed in March of 1807, Congress gave the traders nine months to close down their human trafficking operations. After January 1 of 1808, it would "not be lawful to import or bring into the United States or the territories thereof from any foreign kingdom, place, or country, any Negro, mulatto, or person of color, with intent to hold, sell, or dispose of such [person] ... as a slave, to be held to service or labor" (Schomburg Center). The act provided an enormous penalty up to $20,000 to be imposed on anyone building a ship for the trade or fitting out an existing ship to be used in the trade (Schomburg Center). This act merely cut off the import of new slaves and did not consent to freeing the Blacks that were already in the United States. Slaves were still being traded within the states themselves. The act began a series of events that eventually led to the freeing of Blacks, but the struggle was far from over as the economic outlook for America changed.

Between years 1800 and 1860, the Industrial Revolution transformed the northern part of America, but it had very little effect on the Southern States. The Southerners were convinced that the enslavement of African Americans needed to be continued for their economic prosperity. By 1840, the cotton crops produced in the Southern States earned more money than all other U.S. exports combined. Southerners stuck to their belief that cotton could only be grown with slave labor. Over time many took for granted that their prosperity, even their way of life, was inseparable from African American slavery. The Southern States continued heavy reliance on agriculture with little regard for industry. By 1850 the debate over slavery had the Northern Industrialists and the Southern Agriculturalists divided over their different points of view. The plantation owners still depended on the slave labor to plant, maintain, and harvest their crops. Abolitionists sought to end the enslavement of African Americans and pressured Government officials to follow suit. This initiated the talk of the Southern States seceding from the union. Attitudes in the two sections of the nation continued to harden into the late 1850s. Abolitionists continued to file petitions calling for basic human rights but continued to meet resistance even in the judicial courts. An example was the 1857 decision by the Supreme Court in the Dred Scott case. The Court ruled that Americans of African descent were not U.S. citizens (Interior). Dred Scott was a slave who had lived in the free State of Illinois and the free Territory of Wisconsin. Before he moved back to the slave State of Missouri where he was originally from, he filed an appeal to the Supreme Court in hopes of being granted his freedom (Bank.WBGH, PBS Online Part 4, 2013). Cases such as this and a failed effort to start a slave uprising in Virginia by abolitionist John Brown in 1859 spread fear and distress across the South (Interior). That fear only sparked more hatred for the African American race among White Americans and resulted in a rise in the violence against Blacks.

The Southern States were preparing to guard their way of life against the U.S. Government and foresaw the upcoming presidential elections of 1860 as a strike against them. Public debates by politicians such as Illinois Abraham Lincoln and a popular Senator named Stephen A. Douglas got national attention. Lincoln's political profile grew in popularity with him openly opposing slavery, and he was thrust into the election of 1860 as the Republican Party's Presidential Candidate. Prior to the 1860 election, the Democratic Party split into two factions. The Northern Democrats nominated Lincoln's rival, Senator Stephen Douglas. The Southern Democrats nominated John C. Breckenridge, the incumbent vice president, and a pro-slavery man from Kentucky (McNamara).

In November of 1860, Abraham Lincoln was elected President of the United States. President Lincoln was opposed to the expansion of slavery, but his election alone escalated the call for the Southern States' secession. (Darlene Clark Hine, p. 228) President Lincoln swept the vote in the Northern States by running on a ticket which called for keeping slavery out of the new territories and ending slavery (Interior). South Carolina saw Lincoln's election for what it was, an act to abolish slavery. As a result, South Carolina became the first of seven states to secede from the Union in 1860. It was followed by Mississippi, Alabama, Florida, Louisiana, Georgia, and Texas. During the four months leading up to Lincoln's Inauguration, the seceding states, one after another, seized federal forts, arsenals, and customs houses within their borders. There was little to oppose the breakaway forces, but a caretaker and a guard or two which comprised many of the garrisons. On March 4, 1861, Lincoln was inaugurated, promising the seceding states that he would use force only "to hold, occupy, and possess the property and places" belonging to the federal government which set the stage for war" (Jenkins, 2011).

In April 1861, the confederates demanded the surrender of Fort Sumter in Charleston, South Carolina. The commander refused and the confederates delivered the first blow and began the Civil War by firing artillery on Fort Sumter. Shortly after that initial conflict, four more states seceded; Virginia, North Carolina, Arkansas, and Tennessee (Jenkins, 2011). The conflict was not about African Americans initially. Neither the North nor the South sought to change the social status of African Americans or free slaves. It was a White man's war waged by the South in order to establish an independent nation that would be free to promote slavery, and the North noted that they fought to preserve the Union, not to free African Americans.

President Lincoln began to shift his attention more toward slavery and initially proposed African American emancipation with compensation and colonization outside of the country in 1862. That proposal was strongly rejected and was seen as a racial change to society. Not until the summer of 1862 did Lincoln again discuss freeing slaves (Darlene Clark Hine, p. 239). In late September he issued a preliminary proclamation. The proclamation called for anyone in bondage to be free if the states had not rejoined the union by 1863; but if they rejoined, slavery would be maintained. President Lincoln's main objective was to preserve the union at any cost (Darlene Clark Hine, p. 240). By January of 1863, Lincoln issued the Emancipation Proclamation. It had little impact initially, but it turned the Civil War into a war about freeing African American slaves (Darlene Clark Hine, p. 241).

Throughout the war, Black men fought on both sides. The South, however, considered a Black man in a confederate uniform to be against the laws of nature and what they stood for. But with a failing government and poorly manned army, the South not only decided to enlist Black men, but also provided them with equal pay as well. By the time they could recruit and organize Black companies to fight, General Robert E. Lee surrendered to General Ulysses S. Grant at the Appomattox Courthouse in April of 1865 (Darlene Clark Hine, p. 256). The surrender ended the Civil War, and shortly afterward Congress ratified of the Thirteenth Amendment to the Constitution in December of 1865. These events birthed a new challenge for Americans, Black and White alike. Two hundred and fifty years of enslavement had ended and a new chapter began for African Americans.

This new freedom meant families had hopes of being re-united and that women and children could no longer be sold and sexually exploited. It meant that Blacks had the right to an education, to own their own land and earn a living. It was a traumatic experience for many plantation owners and began an entirely new movement against Black equality. White Americans were not ready for blacks to intermingle in their society. Hate groups such as the Klu Klux Klan were formed, and the enactment of the Jim Crow laws creating the separate but equal conditions still denied Blacks complete freedom. The Klan and hate was fueled by a widespread fear among many Southern Whites of an insurrection by former slaves. Intimidation, lynching, and violence started just eight months after the civil war ended. The groups consisted of mostly former confederate soldiers (Klu Klux Klan 1868, 2006). Despite the major improvements, life for Southern blacks was far from perfect. "Black Codes" were also enacted and designed to limit the opportunities of Blacks in the South during Reconstruction. The Black Codes placed taxes on free blacks who tried to pursue nonagricultural professions, restricted the abilities of blacks to rent land or own guns, and even allowed the children of "unfit" parents to be apprenticed to the old slave masters (Cozzens, 1998).

Even though nearly all the doors were closed to Blacks during this era in America, they still made their presence known. Black men plowed fields, built buildings, filed petitions, preached religious sermons, published literature, and even fought in the American Wars (Darlene Clark Hine). African Americans began to influence the United States of America even before it declared its independence from the British and continue to influence America today. For over 300 years Africans have adapted to the land and the American way of life, excelling in every area in society from slavery to now.

CHAPTER II

• • •

Scholars

Throughout the troubling times of African Americans, some Black men have led the way in education among the others. Accounts of African Americans in schools date as far back as the early 1700s. Black children, born enslaved and free alike, were taught by European settlers in their schools alongside White children. In a few instances, religious groups would establish schools for Black and Indian children which would often meet two to three times a week and were generally located near the church (University, 2011). They would spend shorter hours in school during the harvest and planting seasons because the labor was more significant than a slave acquiring an education.

Most farmers taught their children to read and write at home using a bible and a hornbook. A hornbook was a wooden board with a handle with a lesson sheet of the ABCs in small and capital letters, a series of syllables, and a copy of the Lord's Prayer attached. Wealthier families constructed cabins with single chalkboards and were able to hire teachers to instruct their children. They used books and instructed in the 3 Rs (Reading, Writing, and 'Rithmetic) (Library, 2013). These lessons were taught exclusively to the upper class to allow them to maintain power, be scholarly, and manage their money (University, 2011). By the 1750s, literacy rates were the highest in the New England colonies, at about 75% for males and 65% for females. The literacy rates, however, were lower in the Middle and Southern colonies (Library, 2013). As a result of the industrial revolution, many new jobs were available, which made education more popular and drew in many farmers. Well after the revolution began, the government began to pass laws stating that townships should have public schools (University, 2011).

The shift from servitude to enslavement and the start of racial divide soon caused White Americans to shun Blacks from their institutions. It was not until after the American Revolution that several literary societies and African American schools began to emerge (Williams A. H., 2004). Prior to the establishment of those schools many Blacks had to use ingenuity to simply learn to speak the new language and eventually learn to read and write it. They used skills such as active listening, which required them to listen with great attention. They would later take what they heard and say it repetitively until they got the full understanding of the words they heard. This was a general practice among the Blacks who worked in close proximity to Whites that would often read aloud and converse in front of them (Williams A. H., 2004).

In the year 1800, many Blacks had already gained their freedom in the Northern New England States, and nearly three-quarters had gained their freedom by 1810. However, with the growing consciousness of skin color, free Blacks only received a ranking of second-class citizenship.

In the South, where slavery provided the economic foundation, nearly the entire African American population remained slaves (Darlene Clark Hine). Fearing that Black literacy would pose a threat to the slave system, many colonies developed laws to prevent slaves from learning to read and write (PBS Online, 2013). One example of these laws would be the South Carolina Act of 1740, which read:

Whereas, the having slaves taught to write, or suffering them to be employed in writing, may be attended with great inconveniences; Be it enacted, that all and every person and persons whatsoever, who shall hereafter teach or cause any slave or slaves to be taught to write, or shall use or employ any slave as a scribe, in any manner of writing whatsoever, hereafter taught to write, every such person or persons shall, for every such offense, forfeit the sum of one hundred pounds, current money. (PBS Online, 2013)

Most slave States developed similar laws prohibiting the education of blacks, like this revised version of Virginia's Slave Code published in 1812, it read:

That all meetings or assemblages of slaves, or free negroes or mulattoes mixing and associating with such slaves at any meeting-house or houses, &c., in the night; or at any school or schools for teaching them reading or writing, either in the day or night, under whatsoever pretext, shall be deemed and considered an unlawful assembly; and any justice of a county, &c., wherein such assemblage shall be, either from his own knowledge or the information of others, of such unlawful assemblage, &c., may issue his warrant, directed to any sworn officer or officers, authorizing him or them to enter the house or houses where such unlawful assemblages, &c., may be, for the purpose of apprehending or dispersing such slaves, and to inflict corporal punishment on the offender or offenders, at the discretion of any justice of the peace, not exceeding twenty lashes. (PBS Online, 2013)

Despite the laws and customs in America that prohibited African Americans from learning to read and write, a few managed to acquire some degree of literacy and even excel to become scholars (Williams A. H., 2004, p. 7). Enslaved African American's ability to learn in private demonstrated how they often undermined the master-slave relationship. The ability to read gave African Americans the ability to see beyond the institution of slavery. Being literate gave slaves hopes of being free. African Americans and White abolitionists in the New England States drafted petitions for freedom and began releasing black publications calling for the abolition of slavery (Williams A. H., 2004). These publications fueled slave defiance and escapes.

The spread of education among Blacks was on the rise with the help of Freed African societies, White abolitionists, and concerned individuals. Two of the most notable African American men that contributed to the beginning of widespread literacy among African Americans were Richard Allen and Prince Hall.

Richard Allen, a minister and educator, was born a slave in Pennsylvania in 1760. As a young teen, he began to follow the teachings of the Methodist Church. He began to Minster to his owner and fellow slaves, teaching them that on judgment day slaveholders would be weighed in the balance. He instilled enough guilt in his owner that he was able to buy his freedom during the Revolutionary era. Once Allen was free, he began a traveling ministry stretching from New York to the Carolinas. He eventually settled in Philadelphia where he was appointed to the position of Associate Minister in a racially mixed St. George Methodist Church in 1786. Strong followers motivated Allen into establishing his own church for Blacks in 1787 (Henretta, 1997). His establishment was called the African Methodist Episcopal Church, which currently has membership in twenty Episcopal Districts, thirty-nine countries located on five continents (General Secretary, 2013). In 1795, he opened a day school for sixty children and in 1804 founded the "Society of Free People of Color for Promoting the Instruction and School Education of Children of African Descent." By 1811, there were less than 11 black schools in the city of Philadelphia. Allen learned to live as a free Black man in White America, rejecting emigration and preserving his cultural identity by creating separate African-American institutions of learning (Henretta, 1997).

Prince Hall, during the Revolutionary period, was considered one of Boston's most prominent citizens. He was born a slave in 1735, in Boston. Not much was known of his youth, but shortly after the Boston Massacre Hall was granted his freedom. His freedom certificate stated that; "Prince Hall was no longer reckoned a slave, but [had] always accounted as a free man" (PBS Online, 2013). Hall earned his living as a caterer and leather craftsman. Military records account for six soldiers named Prince Hall in the Battle of Bunker Hill. It is believed that he was one of the six black men of Massachusetts listed in the Revolution. A bill he sent to a Colonel Crafts company indicated that he crafted five leather drumheads for the Boston Regiment of Artillery in April 1777 (PBS Online, 2013).

Hall and fourteen other free blacks joined a British lodge of Masons in 1775. After the British left, they formed the first African American Lodge which became the first society in American history devoted to social, political, and economic improvement (PBS Online, 2013). Hall was active in Boston's black community and publicly called for the abolition of slavery and rights for blacks. He focused his energy the education of black children. Dissatisfied by the lack of schools for black children, he eventually established one in his own home (PBS Online, 2013).

Prince Hall's legacy lives on through the African American Free Masons across the country. The organization now manages Scholarship funds such as The Prince Hall Memorial Scholarship, which collects and distributes grants and scholarships to deserving low-income minority students, children of members of the Prince Hall family, and other high school seniors, who have demonstrated a desire to achieve in spite of their economic circumstances (Masons, 2014).

The spread of education could not be stopped. Despite the struggle, African American scholars emerged throughout the continuing history of African Americans. Four of the most notable scholars early on were Fredrick Douglass, Booker T. Washington, William E.B. Dubois, and George Washington Carver.

Frederick Douglass was born a slave in the year 1818, in Maryland. When Douglass was around eight years old his owner's wife taught him the alphabet. She continued to teach young Douglass until her husband prohibited her from doing so. By this time, there were laws against educating slaves with harsh penalties as I mentioned earlier (Fremarjo Enterprises, Inc, 2011). This did not stop young Douglass from soliciting the help of the white children he grew up around. At the age of twelve, Frederick Douglass purchased a popular textbook used in White schools titled "The Columbian Orator" by Caleb Bingham. The book gave instructions on public speaking and had a collection of examples of political dialogues, essays, and speeches. Douglass credits this book with giving him an appreciation for the power words could have. He continued to self-educate by becoming an avid reader (Fremarjo Enterprises, Inc, 2011).

At the age of fifteen, Douglass became a field hand where he was exposed to the physical and mental abuse most slaves endured. While on the plantation, he taught other slaves to read the New Testament by hosting weekly church services

(Fremarjo Enterprises, Inc, 2011). His owner did not intervene with the service, but other slave owners disbanded the gatherings permanently by forming a mob and threatening them with violence. In 1838, at the age of twenty, Douglass escaped slavery with the aid of his future wife Anna Murray and the Underground Railroad (Fremarjo Enterprises, Inc, 2011).

Douglass and his wife settled in New Bedford, Massachusetts, which was a thriving black community. He began attending abolitionist meetings and became active in the community (Biography.com, 2013). He started telling his story of growing up as a slave at the meetings, which thrust him into becoming a regular anti-slavery speaker. His first autobiography, "Narrative of the Life of Frederick Douglass, an American Slave," was published in 1845. It became a bestseller in the U.S. and was also published in several European languages (Biography.com, 2013). Critics spoke out against the former slave with no formal education and immediately attempted to discredit his work. They also brought attention to Douglass' status as a runaway slave (Biography.com, 2013).

Despite the work of his critics, Douglass went on to publish two more versions of his autobiography, and two years later Frederick Douglass purchased his freedom with the help of some Irish and British supporters (Biography.com, 2013). Douglass then began to produce some abolitionist newspapers: The North Star, the Frederick Douglass Weekly, the Frederick Douglass' Paper, the Douglass' Monthly, and the New National Era.

In 1848 Douglass aided in the movement for women's rights, and by the Civil War Douglass was considered the most famous African American man in the country. He consulted with President Abraham Lincoln on the treatment of Black Soldiers and the Emancipation Proclamation (Biography.com, 2013). After the war, he was appointed to several political positions. He served as president of the

Freedman's bank, was placed in charge of U.S. affairs with the Dominican Republic, and was later appointed Consul-General to the Republic of Haiti (Biography.com, 2013).

Douglass' involvement in politics continued. Victoria Woodhull of the Equal Rights Party placed Douglass as a running mate for Vice President of the United States in 1872 (Biography.com, 2013). Douglass never campaigned, but it marked the first time that an African American appeared on a presidential ballot (Biography.com, 2013). Douglass continued on holding several political offices, such as U.S. Marshall of the District of Columbia and U.S. Minister to Haiti. He died in 1895 after a life of activism dedicated to the advancement of Black people.

His legacy lives on through programs such as The Douglass Scholars Program, presented by Fred Morsell through the Fremarjo Enterprises Corporation. This program gives young people information and understanding which encourages them to draw on their personal resources to overcome the doubts, fears, and prejudices that contribute to the belief that they cannot fully participate in all of society's opportunities (Fremarjo Enterprises, Inc, 2011).

Booker T. Washington was born a slave in 1856 in Franklin County Virginia. Washington often stared into the windows of the schoolhouse near the plantation and would watch the White children sitting at their desks reading books. This sparked his interest in education (A & E Networks LLC, 2013). At the age of nine, following the Civil War, his mother moved to West Virginia. Booker still had to work in order to help support the family. His mother did embrace his desire to learn and purchased Washington a book so he could learn the alphabet and eventually learn to read and write. His desire to learn was so strong that he woke up at 4 a.m. to read and study (A & E Networks LLC, 2013). In 1866, he went to work for a coal miner's wife who also saw his desire for education and recognized his intelligence. Washington was allowed to go to school for an hour a day during the winter months. In 1872, at the age of 16, Washington left home and walked some five hundred miles to the Hampton Norman Agricultural Institute (A & E Networks LLC, 2013). He convinced the administrators to let him attend school and work as a janitor to help pay his tuition. His hard work soon earned him a scholarship. The school's headmaster was a former Union officer who commanded a Black Regiment during the Civil War. He strongly supported the education of newly freed slaves (A & E Networks LLC, 2013). After graduating with honors, Booker began to teach in his hometown of Malden, Virginia and continued his education at Wayland Seminary in Washington, D.C. In 1879, he was asked to speak at the Hampton graduation ceremony where he once again impressed the Headmaster who in turn offered Booker a position. Two years later the Alabama legislature approved $2,000 to open a school for blacks in Tuskegee. The school was to be modeled after the Hampton Normal Institute and named the Tuskegee Norman Agricultural and Industrial Institute (today's Tuskegee University) (A & E Networks LLC, 2013). The Headmaster was asked to recommend a White male to run the school, but instead he recommended Booker T. Washington. Strange enough, he reassured Whites that nothing in the Tuskegee program would threaten White supremacy or pose any economic competition to Whites (A & E Networks LLC, 2013).

Under Washington, Tuskegee became one of the leading schools in the country. When Washington died in November of 1915, the institute had an enrollment of 1500 students, over 200 faculty teaching 38 different trades and professions, and a nearly 2 million dollar endowment (A & E Networks LLC, 2013). Washington developed the curriculum, highlighting the virtues of patience, enterprise, and thrift. He believed that economic success for Blacks was a process which required Blacks to remain subordinate to Whites. He felt it was necessary until African Americans could earn full economic and political rights. Hard work was the means to obtaining financial independence and cultural advancement, thus winning acceptance and respect from the white community (A & E Networks LLC, 2013).

In 1895, Booker T. Washington had the opportunity to share his philosophy on race relations. He gave a speech known as the "Atlanta Compromise" at the Cotton States and International Exposition in Atlanta, Georgia. In his speech Washington stated, "that African Americans should accept disenfranchisement and social segregation as long as whites allow them economic progress, educational opportunities, and justice in the courts" (A & E Networks LLC, 2013). Parts of the African American community disagreed, primarily in the North. Activists such as William Edward Burghardt Dubois criticized Washington's philosophy. He disagreed with Washington for not demanding equality for African Americans as granted by the 14th Amendment, which resulted in Dubois becoming an advocate for full and equal rights in every realm of a person's life (A & E Networks LLC, 2013). Washington's philosophy and approach to Black equality conflicted with the aggressive nature of Dubois (NAACP, 2013). The openly publicized views of these great scholars led to intellectual debates that have lasted into today.

William Edward Burghardt Dubois, better known as W. E. B. Dubois, was born on February 23, 1868 in Massachusetts. Historians believed there were somewhere between twenty five to fifty Black people in the community of 5000 during that time (Hynes, 1974). He grew up with very little exposure to racism. The community began to adopt the racism theory of inequality and over time changed his personality from being a good-natured, outgoing person to a withdrawn, grim individual. Years of being subjected to suggestive innuendoes and vindictive attitudes from White Americans changed Dubois and haunted him throughout his life (Hynes, 1974).

Dubois was a gifted intellectual and stood out among the other students during his high school years. He showed concern for his race as early as age fifteen. He became a correspondent for the New York Globe, which he used to motivate other Blacks to move forward. He gave lectures and by published editorials urging Black people to get involved in their community and politics (Hynes, 1974). After graduating high school with honors, he longed to attend the prestigious Harvard University. Dubois did not have the financial support to attend Harvard but settled for a scholarship to Fisk College. His family and friends pooled together to assist young Dubois to continue his education (Hynes, 1974).

Dubois arrived at Fisk College in Nashville, Tennessee in 1885. It was during his college years in Tennessee that he was exposed to discrimination in unimaginable ways and became even more determined to expedite the emancipation of his people. With his personality darkened by this exposure, Dubois became even more motivated to become a writer, editor, and a public speaker for the advancement of Colored people. While at Fisk, Dubois spent two summers teaching at a county school in order to learn more about the South and his people. There, he learned first-hand of poverty, poor land conditions, ignorance, and prejudice. But most importantly, he learned that his people had a deep desire for knowledge (Hynes, 1974).

In 1889, Dubois entered Harvard as a junior with the aid of some scholarships and graduated cum laude with a bachelor's of arts in 1990 (NAACP, 2013). He immediately began graduate work focused on philosophy and centered in history but eventually turned toward economics and social problems. He completed his masters in the spring of 1891 and set his gaze upon a doctorate. Before Dubois completed his masters, the ex-president Rutherford B. Hayes, the current head of a fund to educate Negroes, was quoted in the Boston Herald as claiming that they could not find one worthy enough for advanced study abroad (Hynes, 1974). Dubois' anger inspired him to apply directly to Hayes. His credentials and references were so impeccable that he not only received a grant, but also a letter from Hayes stating that he had been misquoted. Dubois accepted the grant to study in Germany at the University of Berlin. It was considered to be one of the world's finest institutions of higher learning, and Dubois felt that a doctoral degree would further prepare him for his life's work (Hynes, 1974).

While in Berlin, Dubois began to see the race problems in the Americas, Africa, and Asia, and the political development of Europe as one. "This was the period of his life that united his studies of history, economics, and politics into a scientific approach of social research" (Hynes, 1974). Adversity was still an obstacle even at that level of education. Dubois completed a draft of his dissertation and needed another semester to finish his degree when the men over his funding source decided that the education he was learning what he needed to help Negroes (Hynes, 1974). He was asked to return and complete his education at Harvard University. This act did not hurt Dubois but placed him where he wanted to be. He wrote his doctoral thesis on, The Suppression of the African Slave Trade in America. That thesis remains the most authoritative work on that subject and is the first volume in Harvard's Historical Series (Hynes, 1974).

Dubois was certain that the race problem was one of ignorance and was determined to provide a cure for color prejudice. His studies led into a historical investigation, a statistical measurement, and a sociological interpretation of Blacks. His work was published in The Philadelphia Negro. The work changed the way Blacks were viewed. It revealed that Blacks were not just apt to commit crime and would go to great lengths to develop as a society and strive for equality. His works led him to be known as the father of Social Science. After the completion of the study, Dubois accepted a position at Atlanta University to further his research and teachings in sociology. According to Hynes, "for thirteen years, Dubois wrote and studied Negro morality, urbanization, Negroes in business, college-bred Negroes, the Negro church, and Negro crime" (Hynes, 1974). Dubois' work was brilliant and so thorough that every study of the African American race since has some degree of dependence on his investigations.

Dubois' work was relentless. He published several works such as The Souls of Black Folks and the Crisis magazine. The Crisis magazine was the principle publication for distributing NAACP policy and news concerning Blacks (Hynes, 1974). Dubois also wrote two novels, The Quest of the Silver Fleece in 1911 and Dark Princess: A Romance in 1928; a book of essays and poetry, Darkwater: Voices from within the Veil in 1920; and two histories of black people, The Negro in 1915 and The Gift of Black Folk: Negroes in the Making of America in 1924 (NAACP, 2013). From 1934 to 1944 Dubois was chairman of the department of sociology at Atlanta University. Black Reconstruction in America, 1860-1880 in 1935, was one of his most significant historical works and detailed the role of African Americans in American society (NAACP, 2013). In 1940, he also founded a social science quarterly called, Phylon. These are only a few of his many publications.

Dubois died in 1963, in Ghana on the eve of the civil rights march in Washington D.C. Dubois' most lasting contribution is his writing. As a poet, playwright, novelist, essayist, sociologist, historian, and journalist, he wrote 21 books, edited 15 more, and published over 100 essays and articles (NAACP, 2013). He is honored today with scholarship programs and was one of the outstanding African American intellectuals of his period in America.

During this same period in time, another Black scholar emerged named **George Washington Carver.** He was born a slave in Missouri around 1864. The exact date is unknown. After the Civil War, his owners decided to keep the young Carver and his brother to raise and educate. He graduated high school but was denied admittance to Highland College in Highland, Kansas. George found acceptance in Simpson College of arts and later studied at Iowa Agricultural University where he studied botany. Carver chose a career of teaching and research after graduating from Iowa State. He went on to become one of Americas leading inventors, botanists, and chemists. Booker T. Washington, over the African-American Tuskegee Institute, hired Carver to chair the school's agricultural department in 1896 (Biography. com, 2013). Carver's research in plant biology brought him and Tuskegee national recognition. His research focused on new uses for crops such as peanuts, sweet potatoes, soybeans and pecans. The hundreds of products he invented included plastics, paints, dyes and even a kind of gasoline. To many Blacks, Carver's life demonstrated the transforming potential of education, even for those born into the most unfortunate and difficult of circumstances (Biography.com, 2013).

These gentlemen set the stage and led the way for the African American scholars today. Their quest for knowledge demonstrated that African Americans could be educated and excel even through the adverse times in America. There are several notable scholars today working toward not only the equality of Africans Americans but throughout all aspects of society.

Some more modern scholars that excelled in their respective fields are Dr. Percy Julian and Dr. Keith Black.

Dr. Percy Julian was a pioneering chemist whose parents were former slaves in Montgomery, Alabama (Biography. com, 2013). He was born in 1899 and attended a segregated school for Black children up to the eighth grade. He was not allowed to attend high school with the Whites in the area, and there was no high school for Blacks. This did not stop Percy from seeking a higher education. He applied to DePauw University in Greencastle, Indiana. He had to take high school level classes in the evenings with his freshman and sophomore course load. Despite being born in a racially charged environment and behind his peers in education, he graduated first in his class with honors (Biography.com, 2013).

Julian accepted a position as a chemistry instructor at Fisk University after graduating college. Julian was awarded the Austin Fellowship in Chemistry while at Fisk. He later moved to the distinguished Harvard University in Cambridge, Massachusetts where he excelled at the graduate level. (Adscape International, LLC, 2011). He received a master's degree in 1923, finishing at the top of his class (Adscape International, LLC, 2011). Despite being a distinguished graduate, Julian was unable to obtain a position as a teaching assistant at any major university because of the color of his skin. University leaders believed that White students would refuse to take instruction from a Black professor, so Julian accepted a position at the West Virginia State College Blacks and soon moved to Washington D.C. to become an associate professor of chemistry at Howard University. He remained at Howard for two years before obtaining his Ph.D. at the University of Vienna in Austria in 1931 (Adscape International, LLC, 2011).

Julian returned to the United States and moved back to DePauw where he was appointed a teacher in organic chemistry, which is where he discovered physostigmine, a drug used to treat glaucoma. Julian received international recognition and was approached by the Dean of the University to possibly become the next Chair over the chemistry department. He was not awarded the position because of his race and a concern for the possible reaction of white students (Adscape International, LLC, 2011). In late 1935, Percy Julian entered the corporate world by accepting a position at the Glidden Company as chief chemist and the Director of the Soya Product Division (Adscape International, LLC, 2011).

On December 24, 1935, Percy married Anna Johnson and the couple settled into a comfortable life in Chicago. Percy then developed a way to inexpensively produce male and female hormones from soybeans. These hormones helped to prevent miscarriages and later aided in the fight against cancer and other ailments. He later invented a synthetic version of cortisone, which greatly relieved the pain of rheumatoid arthritis. All-natural cortisone was extremely expensive and only wealthy people could afford it. His work was so brilliant that in 1950 the City of Chicago named him Chicagoan of the Year. The honor did not gain him acceptance by his white counterparts in his field or in his community. Soon after he purchased a home for his family in nearby Oak Park, it was set on fire on Thanksgiving Day in 1950. One year later, dynamite was thrown in front of his home from a passing car. Even though his work relieved the pain of many of people in Oak Park, some still could not stand to have him as their neighbor just because he was Black (Adscape International, LLC, 2011).

Julian left Glidden in 1953 and established his own laboratory, Julian Laboratories, in 1954. He sold the company in 1961, becoming one of the first black millionaires, before founding Julian Research Institute, a nonprofit organization that he ran until 1975 when he passed away from liver cancer.

Dr. Keith Black was born in 1957, in Tuskegee, Alabama. "Though the Supreme Court had declared school segregation unconstitutional years before Keith Black was born, the state government of Alabama continued to mandate separate schools for black and white children" (Museum of Living History, 2010). His parents were teachers, and his father, a principal who hired a segregated staff encouraged young Keith (Museum of Living History, 2010). He developed a fascination with biology and even taught himself how to dissect a frog. His father purchased a cow's heart to show support for Keith's growing fondness for science and eventually moved the family to Ohio for better schools (Museum of Living History, 2010).

Keith joined an apprentice program at Case Western Reserve University to learn basic laboratory skills. While still in high school, he took a part-time job at Cleveland's St. Luke's Hospital. Frederick Cross and Richard Jones, inventors of the Cross-Jones artificial heart valve, hired him as an assistant to work in their lab. He learned to perform transplant surgeries and heart valve replacements on laboratory dogs. It was during that time he observed the processed damaged red blood cells in patients with heart valve replacements. Those observations formed a basis of Black's first scientific paper, which he published at age 17. His paper won the Westinghouse Science Award, a research-based science competition in the United States for high school seniors. The Westinghouse Award has been referred to as, "the nation's oldest and most prestigious science competition" (National Academy of Sciences, 2013).

Keith entered the University of Michigan after high school and completed an accelerated college program, earning his undergraduate and medical degrees in just six years. He completed his internship in general surgery and residency in neurological surgery at the University of Michigan Medical Center (National Academy of Sciences, 2013). He began successful research by designing ways to open blood-brain barriers which enables chemotherapeutic drugs to be delivered directly into tumors. Dr. Black also conducted ground-breaking research which led to the development of a vaccine that enhances the body's immune response to brain tumors. He also used gene arrays to develop molecular profiles of tumors, employed optical technology for brain mapping, and learned how to destroy brain tumors with focused microwave energy (National Academy of Sciences, 2013).

The handful of specialized brain tumor surgeons in the United States perform fewer than 100 surgeries a year. Keith Black typically performs over 200 in a given year. In the first two decades of his career he performed well over 5,000 such operations. In many cases, Dr. Black has saved the lives of patients that other surgeons believed were inoperable (Museum of Living History, 2010). Dr. Black continues to do research focused on the human brain.

These scholars have defied the odds to obtain an education and used it to excel above others and to make major contributions to society. From slavery to now, Black men have survived the harsh conditions the African American race was subjected to. Early settlers passed acts to prevent the education of any person of color. Those acts evolved into the Jim Crow laws, separate but equal.

According to research by Huffington Post, "more than half the young black men who graduated high school in 2010 earned their diploma in four years, which was an improved graduation rate that still lagged behind that of their white counterparts" (Gambao, 2012). The Schott Foundation for Public Education, which has tracked graduation rates of black males from U.S. public schools since 2004, found "that 52 percent of black males who entered high school in the 2006-07 school years, graduated in four years compared to 78 percent of white males and 58 percent of Latino males." The foundation releases its report every two years and by 2008; the black male graduation rate was down to 47 percent (Washington, 2012). Huffington Post also discovered that:

The national college graduation rate for black men is 33.1 percent. Black men represent 7.9 percent of 18-to-24-year-olds in America but only 2.8 percent of undergraduates at public flagship universities. The national college graduation rate for Hispanic men is 41.1 percent and for Native Americans and Alaska natives 33.8 percent. In comparison, the graduation rate for white males is 54.5 percent. Asian/Pacific Islanders have the highest rate, 60.6 percent. (Gambao, 2012)

As the statistics show, Black males are making small improvements in the amount of graduates of high school and college. The challenges Blacks faced in early America are not as prominent today, however the struggle is not over. Today there are thousands of scholarships and grants being offered by various organizations that are dedicated specifically for the education and advancement of Black people. The opportunity is there if one chooses to seek an education today.

CHAPTER III

• • •

Religious Leaders

Africans arrived in America with a belief in a higher God who created all things. They also believed in lesser gods who followed that high God. They prayed and offered sacrifices to the lesser gods when dealing with rain, fertility, and crops. Status with the lesser gods was important to Africans because they believed they were occupied by the spirits of their ancestors (Perez, 2013). Their beliefs in status guided them to honor their ancestors, recognize the lesser gods, and give all power and praise to the higher God. In this chapter I will give you an overview of some of the greatest African American religious leaders from origins to present day America.

Enslaved Africans Americans initially resisted giving up the religious beliefs of their forefathers. Over the years with the help of new generations born in American, Christianity became part of accepting America as home (WGBH, 2013). The Christian message was appealing to a large number of slaves. Messages of equality and deliverance among all men before God brought them comfort during those despairing times (WGBH, 2013).

Between 1619 and the early 1700's, slave owners shared conflicting thoughts about converting their slaves into Christians. Some Whites believed that slaves deserved Christian redemption and were not inferior to Whites. Most colonists believed that converting slaves into Christians would cause many problems because of the great number of slaves. They feared Blacks thinking that they were equal to Whites, becoming lazy, or even resisting their White masters (Perez, 2013).

Between 1738 and 1770, missionaries made frequent visits to the Americas seeking to convert as many settlers and slaves as possible. The ministers urged owners to convert the African American slaves to Christianity. Slave owners were told it was their duty to bring their slaves to Christ. The ministers charged the masters with the duty of caring for their slaves in a humane way. They pushed them to develop Christianity among the slaves as a fundamental tenet of the American slave system. The ministers also told the slaves that it was their obligation to be obedient just as they were to God (Slavery and African American Religion, 1997). The missionaries did not tend to challenge the justice of owning slaves but backed the slave system that supplied the white plantations with labor. That labor was critical to the survival of America. They continued these practices up until the revolutionary period. Wave after wave of missionaries and evangelists spread Christianity among White and Black Americans.

Slaves as early as 1774 began petitioning the courts for freedom using Christianity as a stone to strike blows in the minds of law makers. An excerpt from one petition read:

We have in common with all other men a naturel right to our freedoms without being depriv'd of them by our fellow men as we are a freeborn Pepel and have never forfeited this

Blessing by aney compact or agreement whatever. But we were unjustly dragged by the cruel hand of power from our dearest frinds and sum of us stolen from the bosoms of our tender Parents and from a Populous Pleasant and plentiful country and Brought hither to be made slaves for Life in a Christian land. Thus we are deprived of everything that hath a tendency to make life even tolerable, the endearing ties of husband and wife we are strangers to.... By our deplorable situation we are rendered incapable of shewing our obedience to Almighty God how can a slave perform the duties of a husband to a wife or parent to his child How can a husband leave master and work and cleave to his wife How can the wife submit themselves to their husbands in all things. How can the child obey thear parents in all things. There is a grat number of us sencear members of the Church of Christ how can the master and the slave be said to fulfill that command Live in love let Brotherly Love contuner and abound Beare ye onenothers Bordenes. How can the master be said to Beare my Borden when he Beares me down whith the Have chanes of slavery and oppression against my will. (Slavery and African American Religion, 1997)

Religious revivals known as the Great Awakening and the Second Great Awakening shaped American beliefs. From 1740 through 1780 revivals became popular in the North and South. Many Americans, White and Black alike chose to join the Christian movement seeking salvation. The spread of Christianity helped with planning the American Revolution by convincing Americans that they were created equal and should enjoy equal social, political, and economic rights and opportunities (WGBH, 2013).

Slaves converting to Christianity were widespread during the awakening periods, but White owners and churches still thought that slaves were not equal and held segregated religious services and controlled the free worship by slaves.

Some owners would allow slaves to sit in the rear, balcony, or outside the church windows. Research shows that, "African Americans prayed secretly to God as their only master and asked to be liberated from their owners" (Perez, 2013). They reinterpreted Christianity by adding some of their own African religious beliefs. Slaves identified themselves with the Hebrew slaves in the Old Testament as they were liberated by God. African Americans believed that if they prayed hard enough to God that they would be liberated just as the Hebrew slaves were (Perez, 2013). Christianity was a belief in and commitment to a God that helped the poor, judged the arrogant, and punished their owners. They would meet where permitted. They often met in the woods where they believed they were visited by the spirit and engaged in their own song, dance, and praise. Slaves used Christianity in their own terms, such as believing if their masters were not loyal followers of Christianity then the slaves themselves were superior over their masters (Perez, 2013).

African Americans slowly began to take on leadership roles. Those roles would lead to other forms of leadership and protest just as White Americans feared. They rose once again above strong opposition from Whites throughout the colonies. Some of those early leaders were the Reverend Richard Allen whom I mentioned in the previous chapter and Nathaniel "Nat" Turner.

Richard Allen was born a slave on 1760, in Philadelphia and was sold to a farmer in Delaware as a child in 1777. He followed the Methodist teachings of Freeborn Garretson and so did his owner. Garretson converted Allen's master by convincing him that slave owners would be "weighed in the balance on judgment day" (Henretta, 1997). Humbled by his newfound faith, he allowed Allen to buy his freedom. Allen followed his calling by becoming a minister and began preaching to Whites and Blacks along the East Coast from New York to

South Carolina. His work drew the attention of the Methodist Bishop Francis Ashbury who appointed Allen to the position of Assistant Minister in Philadelphia. Once again, he found himself ministering at St. George's Methodist Church to a racially mixed congregation in 1786 (Henretta, 1997). The following year Allen and Absalom Jones, another Black minister, joined freed men, women, and Quakers to begin the Free African Society, an organization that offered fellowship and mutual aid to free African Americans and their descendants.

In early 1794, Allen refused a position in an African Episcopal Church, citing that he preferred to follow the Methodist beliefs. By July of that same year, he decided to form his own church for African Americans. He ministered to ten Black Methodists and converted a blacksmith's shop into the Bethel African Methodist Episcopal Church (Henretta, 1997). By 1795, the Allen's congregation grew to over 120 members and a decade later it had grown to over four hundred and fifty members, when he was ordained as the first Black Deacon of the Methodist Church by Bishop Ashbury in 1799 (Henretta, 1997).

By 1810, the Black population in Philadelphia had reached nearly 10,000 and by 1813 Allen had over 1,200 followers. Free Blacks were attracted to the church's strict system of discipline and its communal sanctions against drinking, gambling, and infidelity. Along with being able to enjoy the full expression of their emotions which had been suppressed by slavery, Allen's teachings helped free Blacks to bring order to their lives (Henretta, 1997).

Reverend Richard Allen died in 1831, but the church he founded stands strong. Currently the African Methodist Episcopal Church has members on five continents, divided into twenty Episcopal Districts, in some thirty-nine countries. It currently list over two and a half million active members in some seven thousand congregations around the world and accepts all races (General Secretary, 2013).

Nathanial Turner, better known as Nat Turner, was born a slave in the year 1800 on a small plantation in Virginia. He took on the last name of his owner, Benjamin Turner which was common in those years. His master's son instructed Turner in reading, writing, and religion. As a small child, Turner was thought to have some unique talent because he could see into the past, recalling events that happened before he was born (A+E Television Networks, LLC., 2013).

His religion grew stronger as he became older. He began to serve as a preacher to the other slaves around him. He spent most of his time reading the Bible, praying, and fasting. Some of the slaves he preached to called him the "prophet" and believed in the visions he spoke of. Turner thought God communicated with him through dreams (Online Highways LLC, 2013).

Turner worked on several plantations before running away from Samuel Turner, his former owner's brother, in 1821. Turner returned to the plantation after hiding for thirty days in the woods and claimed that he received a sign from God. In 1831, after Samuel Turner's death, Nat Turner was sold to the John Travis plantation where he worked until he began the rebellion (A+E Television Networks, LLC., 2013).

Before he was sold in 1825, Turner had a vision of a bloody conflict between light and dark spirits followed by another in 1828. He proclaimed, "the spirit instantly appeared to me and said the Serpent was loosened, and Christ had laid down the yoke he had borne for the sins of men, and that I should take it on and fight against the Serpent" (A+E Television Networks, LLC., 2013). He was to receive another sign to let him know when the fighting should begin, so he began to prepare himself for the battle. Turner intended to slay his enemies with their own weapons (A+E Television Networks, LLC., 2013). He was going to start the rebellion in July of 1831 but fell ill. On August 13, Turner took an atmospheric disturbance in which the sun appeared bluish-green as a sign from God to start his famous Slave Revolt. He started one week later. On August 21, Turner and seven other slaves on the plantation killed John Travis and his family while they slept. Turner then gathered more than 40 or 50 slaves as he and his men continued their murdering spree through Virginia's Southampton County. The revolting slaves killed every White man, woman and child they encountered (A+E Television Networks, LLC., 2013).

His group was finally stopped by an armed mob on the outskirts of a town called Jerusalem. Many of his followers were killed or captured. Turner evaded authorities for six weeks before he was captured, tried, and hanged along with his followers in November of 1831. Nat Turner is considered a hero by many Blacks in America and abroad. No slave revolt in the history of the United States had inflicted such a blow on White slaveholders and their families (Online Highways LLC, 2013). Turner's image has changed over the years. He initially emerged as a hero, a religious fanatic, and then as a villain. Turner became an important icon to the 1960s Black power movement. His rebellion served as an example of how African Americans should stand united against White oppression (A+E Television Networks, LLC., 2013).

These two pre-civil war Black leaders took very different approaches to leading African Americans out of bondage and abolishing slavery. Their courage branched out after the emancipation of Black people and inspired many other Black men to dedicate their lives to spreading religion among African Americans. Several Religious leaders emerged in other religions such as the Catholic and the Baptist Churches. Their most notable were Father Augustine Tolton and Reverend George Liele.

Father Augustine Tolton was born to Peter Paul and Martha Jane Tolton in 1854, in Ralls County, Missouri. His parents were both owned by Catholic families before they got married. Catholics believed in baptizing and teaching their slaves Catholicism. Records show Augustine being baptized the same year he was born at St. Peter's Church at Brush Creek (Catholic Diocese of Memphis, 2011).

The Toltons stayed informed of the political debates over slavery and followed the anti-slavery movement closely. They took an interest in landmark cases such as the famous Dred Scott case, where the Supreme Court ruled that blacks could not be citizens and had no civil rights. After Fort Sumter fell into the hands of the Confederacy, signaling the beginning of the Civil War, Augustine's father escaped to join the union army but died shortly after his escape of dysentery in a St. Louis hospital. Martha, left alone with three children, became desperate to keep the family together and prevent young Augustine from being sold and escaped. They traveled to a community called Quincy some forty miles through fields and dangerous river crossings. The family arrived in Quincy which had work available, schools, several businesses, and churches. Quincy had 25,000 citizens and a Negro district of about 300 Blacks, who offered the family immediate help. Augustine and his brother went to work in a cigar factory alongside their mother (Archdiocese of Chicago, 2013).

Martha Tolton began attending the St. Boniface Church and enrolled Augustine in the school. He was tormented by Whites that were unwilling to accept his presence. Threats against the teachers and priest grew daily, so his mother removed him from the school after only one month. He did manage to learn the German language, which helped him later in life, while attending Mass at the St. Boniface Church. Augustine's education was rocky, he spent only one month at St. Boniface, two months at the Colored School, and three or four years at St. Peter School, but only during the winter months (Archdiocese of Chicago, 2013).

The local priests Father McGirr and Father Schaeffer-meyer called seminaries in the area urging Augustine's acceptance but were turned down, each remarking, "we are not ready for a negro student" each time (Archdiocese of Chicago, 2013). The two priests joined by two other priests made it their mission to educate young Augustine. In 1878, the Franciscans of the St. Francis College hoped Augustine would go to London and study theology when they accepted him as a student. Augustine, however, had his sights set on Rome (Archdiocese of Chicago, 2013). He reported to Seminary school on March 12, 1880. He completed college in two years then completed four years of theological studies and church law. All lectures, textbooks, and examinations were in Latin, which was not a challenge for a well-prepared Augustine. Finally on April 24, 1886 Augustine was ordained by Pope Leo XIII and returned to the United States on July 10 (Archdiocese of Chicago, 2013). Father Tolton's first Mass on American soil took place at the St. Benedict the Moor parish church in New York City. With a congregation of mostly Negroes, the United States celebrated Mass with their first Black ordained priest on July 11, 1886 (Archdiocese of Chicago, 2013). In a speech he delivered in Washington D.C. in 1889, Father Augustine stated, "The Catholic Church deplores double slavery- that of the mind and that of the body. She endeavors to free us of both. I was a poor slave boy, but the priest of the Church did not disdain me. It was through the influence of one of them that I became what I am tonight" (Catholic Diocese of Memphis, 2011).

Father Augustine Tolton eventually returned to Quincy where he held Mass for Black and White congregations. Newspapers reported that the church would often fill to capacity. The school eventually had only Black children enrolled. He passed away in 1897, at 43 years of age with some easily judging that his life was not a success, but

becoming the first African American Priest was no easy
task. His efforts opened the way for thousands of Priest of
African descents (Catholic Diocese of Memphis, 2011).

Reverend George Liele was an enslaved man who
was the first ordained African American Baptist preacher. Liele was born into slavery in Virginia and was owned
by Henry Sharpe, a Baptist deacon. In 1773, Liele joined
the Christian faith at the Buckhead Creek Baptist
Church where he soon began to preach with the permission of Sharpe and the local Baptists (Mickens, 2006).

His owner later allowed Liele to travel to several plantations alongside a White preacher named Wait Palmer. He
ministered and converted several slaves on plantations that
would allow their slaves to receive the Christian message
(Mickens, 2006). One of his converts named David George
joined the two ministers until the approaching war of independence which restricted their travels. Liele left George in
Silver Bluff, South Carolina to reside over a small church
with eight members. This was considered the first established
African American Baptist Church in America (Mickens,
2006). Despite his work as a traveling minister, Liele was
still a slave. He preached at several plantations and converted
countless Blacks to Christianity. In 1775, Liele's owner set
him free. On May 20th of that same year, Liele was ordained
as a minister and became the first ordained African American
Minister and Revivalist in America (Mickens, 2006). Sharpe
died during the Revolutionary War, leaving his property in
the hands of his heirs. Since slaves were considered property,
his heirs wanted to bring Liele back to the plantation to continue work as a slave. During the war, the British controlled
Savannah, so Liele fled the area and began to preach and
baptize African Americans. While traveling and ministering
he met his wife and received credit for establishing two Baptist churches: the First African Baptist Church and the First

Bryan Baptist Church (First African Baptist Church, 2013).

When the British withdrew in 1783, Liele and his family boarded the ship also and found refuge in Jamaica. The tension and demonstration against slavery and the industry had already begun in British ruled Jamaica and Cayman Islands (Gleaner Company, 2013). In 1789, the House of Commons began passing resolutions to combat slavery until it was finally abolished in 1838. To pay for the voyage and refuge, Liele became an indentured servant to General Campbell, the British appointed Governor of Jamaica. Liele labored and earned his family's freedom in less than two years. He became Campbell's minister in his new foreign home and started the first Black Baptist Church with some 350 members (Mickens, 2006). Although he did not return to American soil, his leadership and commitment to better the lives of African Americans through his ministry lives on today.

From early times, African American ministers used religion to unite African Americans by preaching the gospel and establishing places of worship. White America began to tighten its reigns on Blacks by restricting their movement and took away their right to assemble. African American Religious enlightenment carried them through the Civil War era and became a driving force in the Civil Rights movement in 1955-1968.

During the Civil War era, religion aided Blacks by improving morals, escaping bondage, and taught them the benefit of charity and benevolence. It also helped Blacks to deal with uncertainty and find the strength to face persecution and stand together in opposition to slavery and racism (Gourley, 2013). When the Civil War ended, African Americans in the South continued to establish their own churches. With the efforts of northern missionaries, the growth of Black churches started in the South immediately following the Civil War. The churches they established for Black denominations continue to flourish by defying the test of time (Gourley, 2013).

Following the Emancipation, large numbers of Northern Blacks began establishing missions throughout the South to welcome the estimated four million recently freed slaves to the Christian community. Between 1865 and 1900 there was tremendous growth in the Black religious community. Religion was considered a general meeting ground that Blacks could discuss the obstacles they faced becoming citizens. During this era, several ministers began dedicating their life work to bring Black equality to separate but equal America.

There were several Black heroes of ministry known and unknown over the years. There were none more distinguished than Elijah Muhammad and Martin Luther King Junior before and during the Civil Rights Movement. Both men used their influence to further the advancement of Colored people.

Elijah Muhammad was born in Sandersville, Georgia around October 7, 1897. His birthday is unknown because record keeping in Georgia for slaves and their descendants was poorly kept (Nation of Islam, 2013). Elijah (Poole) Muhammad was born the son of a minister, William and Marie Poole, who had 12 other children. Elijah quit school after only reaching the third grade to go to work in the fields to help feed the family (Nation of Islam, 2013).

In April 1923, Elijah moved his family to Detroit, Michigan and went to work at the Cherokee Brick Company. A few years later the stock market crashed, and in 1930, the Great Depression began and racism continued to grow (Nation of Islam, 2013). In the Southern States lynching, race riots, and other forms of terrorism against Blacks continued. Detroit however, with a population of 1.5 million people including some 250,000 Blacks, began to see changes in its social scene (Nation of Islam, 2013).

Elijah's wife learned of a speaker called Master W. Fard Muhammad coming to speak in Detroit on July 4, 1930. He was being called the "Saviour" of Black men and women. Elijah forbid his wife to go for her own safety and went himself to see what the Master had to say (Nation of Islam, 2013). In 1931 Elijah accepted the religion of Islam after hearing just one teaching at the temple. Shortly after accepting the Islam religion he changed his name from his slave master's to Muhammad. He became more involved and received private instruction at the Temple of Islam for 3 years non-stop (Nation of Islam, 2013).

By 1934, Muhammad established a newspaper called, The Final Call to Islam. That same year the Muslim parents with the aid of Elijah established their own schools. They felt the schools in Michigan were inadequate to teach their children properly (Nation of Islam, 2013). Michigan's Board of Education ruled against the Muslims and threw the teachers in jail. The charges were dropped, but Muhammad received a six-month probation period to return the Muslim children to Christian guided schools. Instead of returning the children to public schools he moved to Chicago (Nation of Islam, 2013). The same year the Master was forced out of Detroit and moved to Chicago. By the end of the year, the Master had fled and left Elijah with the mission of saving the Black men and women. Immediately plots to take his life began by members of the Nation of Islam.

Elijah and his family moved to Washington D.C. under different names. He continued to study the Islamic religion as instructed by his mentors (Nation of Islam, 2013). He remained in D.C. until 1942, when he was arrested for avoiding the World War II draft. He claimed, "that he was age 45 and that he would not fight and especially for the infidels" (Nation of Islam, 2013). Muhammad and many of his followers were jailed. He returned to Chicago after he was released (Nation of Islam, 2013).

With Chicago as his new base, Muhammad expanded his membership drive to new heights attracting new members such as Malcolm X and Louis Farrakhan. By 1955, membership had increased but the persecution continued (Nation of Islam, 2013). Members and mosques in the States of Louisiana, California, and Michigan continued to be attacked by White Americans. Anti-Nation of Islam propaganda publicity began to circulate in the media on a large scale. By the early 1960s, the Readers Digest magazine described, "Muhammad as the most powerful Black man in America" (Nation of Islam, 2013).

In 1964, Minister Malcolm X decided to form his own religious and political organization and split from the Nation of Islam (Islam, 2010). He was later killed in a mosque by Muslims while delivering a speech. Elijah Muhammad opened a $2 million mosque and school in Chicago in 1972 (Nation of Islam, 2013). The Nation of Islam grew in all aspects. They owned farms, livestock, grew crops, acquired rental property and began several business ventures (Nation of Islam, 2013). In 1975, the year of Elijah's death, there were more than 75 Nation of Islam Centers in the United States alone.

Elijah Muhammad paved the way for Minister Louis Farrakhan and the present-day Nation of Islam. To date Farrakhan is best known for organizing the Million Man March on Washington D.C. in 1995. The Nation of Islam does not publicly disclose its membership, but it is believed to have some 50,000 core members with unknown amounts of followers in seven countries (Islam, 2010). Under Farrakhan's leadership, the Nation of Islam has established an outpatient clinic for AIDS victims in Washington, D.C. They helped citizens to take back their apartment complexes by forcing drug dealers out of the public and private complexes in the city. In Los Angeles they focused on rehabilitating gang members. Farrakhan and the Nation continued to promote social reform in Black communities by teaching self-reliance and economic independence (Islam, 2010).

Martin Luther King Jr. was born in 1929, on January 15, in Atlanta, Georgia. His parents were the Reverend Martin Luther King, Sr. and Alberta Williams King. King Sr. was the son of a Baptist Minister and his wife was the daughter of sharecroppers (The King Center, 2013). Martin Luther King Jr. went to the separate but equal public schools of Georgia and graduated at the age of fifteen. King received his Bachelor's degree in 1948, from Morehouse College. His father and grandfather were also graduates of the distinguished black school. He attended a predominately White seminary named Crozer in Pennsylvania. He attended for three years and was elected president of his senior class. With the aid of a scholarship he won at Crozer, he entered Boston University where he received his Doctorate degree in 1955. He also met his wife Coretta Scott King while he was in Boston (The King Center, 2013).

In 1954, Martin Luther King began ministering at the Dexter Avenue Baptist Church in Montgomery, Alabama and became a member of the executive committee in the National Association for the Advancement of Colored People (Biography.com, 2013). In December of 1955, he led the first great Black non-violent demonstration in the United States (The Nobel Foundation 1964, 2013). He organized a bus boycott that lasted 382 days during which Dr. King was physically abused, jailed, and had his home bombed (The Nobel Foundation 1964, 2013). The African American community filed a lawsuit against the city arguing that the ordinance was unconstitutional. They based the argument on the Supreme Court's "separate is never equal" decision in Brown v. Board of Education. Montgomery lifted the law mandating segregated public transportation after being defeated in several lower court rulings and suffering large financial losses. This was a huge step for African Americans toward equality (Biography.com, 2013).

In 1957, Martin Luther King Jr. founded the Southern Christian Leadership Conference with the help of sixty other ministers and civil rights activists (The Nobel Foundation 1964, 2013). The Civil Rights leaders felt they needed a national organization in order to unify the power of Black churches. This gave Dr. King national recognition and a wider operating base. The Southern Christian Leadership Conference's first order of business was to get more Blacks involved in the voting process. They began programs to register Blacks to vote across the south, while Dr. King began a series of lectures across the country speaking on race relations. Dr. King also visited India, the birthplace of Gandhi, and was inspired by his teachings of non-violent activism (Biography.com, 2013).

By 1960, African Americans and White activists were staging sit-ins at racially segregated diners. Those sit-ins effectively desegregated business in over 27 cities across the South, but not without a price. Dr. King continued to co-pastor at his father's church in Atlanta, GA. In October of the same year, 75 students were arrested in Atlanta for staging a sit-in at a lunch counter. They were arrested along with Dr. King and 36 other activists. This brought negative attention to the city of Atlanta and caught the attention of President John F. Kennedy. King was soon released after Kennedy made a phone call concerned about Dr. King's harsh treatment (Biography.com, 2013).

In the spring of 1963, Dr. King organized a nonviolent march through the streets in downtown Birmingham, Alabama. The police met the demonstrators with dogs and fire hoses. He was jailed, but the event was broadcast across the nation and throughout the world. From his jail cell, Dr. King publicized his theory of non-violence. He stated, "that non-violent direct action seeks to create such a crisis and foster such a tension that a community, which has constantly refused to negotiate, is forced to confront the issue" (Biography.com, 2013).

By August of 1963, Dr. King and the leaders of the South- ern Christian Leadership Conference had organized a march on Washington D.C. That march drew more than 200,000 people. At the base of the Lincoln Memorial, Dr. King de- livered his famous "I Have A Dream" speech proclaiming, "that someday all men could be brothers" (Biography.com, 2013). These peaceful assemblies spoke volumes to America as a whole and started the nation to question the Jim Crow Laws and the harsh treatment of African Americans. This led to the passing of the Civil Rights Act of 1964, which au- thorized the desegregation of public dwellings and outlawed discrimination in public owned facilities to be enforced by the federal government (The Nobel Foundation 1964, 2013). This also earned Dr. King the Nobel Prize for Peace.

The struggle continued as marchers were being turned away with violence by law enforcement. They were met with vio- lence in 1965 attempting to march from Selma to Montgom- ery, Alabama. The bloody incident was once again broadcast on national television and earned the passing of the Voting Rights Act of 1965 (Biography.com, 2013). Dr. King's unwill- ingness to fight back gained him criticism from some young Black militants who considered it weak not to fight back.

By 1967, Dr. King's vision had expanded, he wanted to form a coalition open to every race in order to address the economic status and unemployment problems of all op- pressed people. In 1968, while planning another march on Washington D.C., Dr. King became distracted by a la- bor strike involving Black sanitation workers in Memphis, Tennessee (The King Center, 2013). He boarded a plane to Memphis, and on April 3, he delivered another power- ful speech to a group of followers gathered at a church. He stated, "I've seen the promised land. I may not get there with you. But I want you to know tonight that we, as a people, will get to the Promised Land" (Biography.com, 2013). The following day he was gunned down while standing on the balcony of the Lorraine Hotel in Memphis, Tennessee by a lone gunman named James Earl Ray (Biography.com, 2013).

Dr. King is still known today as the one who had the greatest impact on race relations in America. He was committed to developing equality for all men with social justice for all. Dr. King is being honored today with a national holiday, with several schools, streets, and public buildings bearing his name, and the recent erection of a memorial on Independence Mall in Washington D.C. (Biography.com, 2013).

The Civil Rights era produced many activists who started as ministers to African Americans that continue the struggle today. Currently Reverend Alfred Charles Sharpton Jr. and Reverend Jesse Jackson continue to lead African Americans in prayer and in the struggle for equality.

Reverend Alfred Sharpton was born in Brooklyn, New York in 1954. His father was a landlord and businessman. His parents divorced when he was nine years old forcing his mother to go on welfare (Biography.com, 2013). He was well-spoken for a child and became well known in the church community at a young age. He was ordained in the Pentecostal Church at the age of 10 and began touring with the celebrity gospel great Mahalia Jackson (Real people For Real Change, 2003). Sharpton was also known to associate with the entertainers James Brown, Michael Jackson, and Don King (Real people For Real Change, 2003). After completing just two years of college he went on the road to organize tours for James Brown.

In 1960, Sharpton became active with the Southern Christian Leadership Conference during the Civil Rights era. He is known for being an outspoken political activist in the fight against racial prejudice and injustices. In 1971, he established the National Youth Movement. He ran for a seat in the New York Senate in 1978, Mayor of New York in 1997, and even became a candidate for Presidency of the United States in 2004.

He continues to bring attention to controversial issues involving social injustice against Blacks (Biography.com, 2013).

Sharpton founded a civil rights organization named the National Action Network in 1991. The organization operates under the same beliefs taught by Dr. Martin Luther King. They promote, "a modern civil rights agenda that includes the fight for one standard of justice, decency and equal opportunities for all people regardless of race, religion, nationality or gender" (National Action Network House of Justice, 2013).

Reverend Jesse Jackson was born October 8, 1941, in Greenville, South Carolina. His father Noah Robinson, a well-known boxer and Helen Burns, who was still in high school, were not married when he was born. His mother did marry one year later to his adoptive father Charles Henry Jackson, a maintenance worker for the postal service (Biography.com, 2013). He was no stranger to racism growing up in segregated Greenville. His elementary school was poorly equipped compared to Whites. Growing up in those conditions, Jackson decide at a young age that; "he was going to be a preacher one day and that he was going to lead people through the rivers of the water" (Biography.com, 2013). Jackson was an exceptional student and athlete. He earned an athletic scholarship to the University of Illinois. He remained only one year and transferred to North Carolina's Agricultural and Technical State University, where he earned a degree in sociology. He began graduate work in theology but did not complete his Masters of Divinity until 2000, but he was ordained by a Baptist church minister in Chicago in 1968 (Biography.com, 2013).

Jackson joined the civil rights movement while in college, and in 1965 he went to Selma, Alabama to march with Dr. Martin Luther King, Jr. He was also present on the balcony when Dr. King was gunned down in Memphis, Tennessee, rendering him aid until the ambulance arrived. In the 1980s, he became African Americans' leading political figure. In 1984, Jesse Jackson became the second African American to make a national run for the Presidency of the United States finishing third with 3.5 million votes. In 1988, Jackson made a second Presidential run, this time he finished second in the democratic primaries to Massachusetts Governor Michael Dukakis. He won more than seven million votes. Jackson was later awarded the 2000 Presidential Medal of Freedom after being appointed special envoy to Africa (Biography.com, 2013).

Jackson declined to run for the presidency a third time, but he did continue to be a force in the political arena. He has continued to push for African American rights and has been invited to be guest speaker at several venues, such as the Democratic Party convention. Jackson founded the Rainbow/People United to Save Humanity foundation in 1971. The foundation, similar to the Southern Christian Leadership Conference's mission, is to assist with the protection of Black homeowners, workers, and businesses. Today the organization's mission is to, "protect, defend, and gain civil rights by leveling the economic and educational playing fields, and to promote peace and justice around the world" (Rainbow/PUSH, 2013). Reverend Jackson continues to fight for social justice through public speaking, hosting debates, and by writing books.

Early settlers debated over teaching slaves religion in the early years and then made laws prohibiting African Americans from being taught. African Americans did not turn away from religion despite the challenges they faced. These well-spoken religious leaders and many that I have failed to mention used religion as a vessel to organize and deliver African Americans out of bondage, and it continues to carry them to an America full of opportunity and equality.

Many emerging Ministers are shadowing the Civil Right era clergy who still bolster large congregations called Mega

Churches. They have membership enrollments that could sway votes in local elections and petition courts such as the 30,000 members of the Potter's Church in Texas and the 25,000 members of the New Birth Missionary Baptist Church in Georgia. These churches are led by charismatic senior pastors, who are active in the community 7 days a week and lead several social and outreach programs.

CHAPTER IV

⋅ ⋅ ⋅

Military Leaders

African American men have played a role in the defense of the United States as early as the prerevolutionary days. Despite arriving in a slave status, African Americans have fought in every American conflict to date. In this chapter I will highlight some heroic Blacks that stepped forward to defend our nation from its early beginnings. These men started a rich tradition of military service and made history along the way. The Revolutionary War was only the beginning of years of Blacks dedicating their lives to defend America. I will also give an overview of notable acts by Blacks in the War of 1812, the Civil War, World War II, the Vietnam War, and Operation Desert Storm.

Crispus Attucks, an escaped slave, may have very well been the first man killed by the British for standing up for America's independence. On March 5 of 1770, the Boston Massacre marked the beginning of the American Revolution. Attucks was not the only American to lose his life when the British fired into the mob, but he was leading the crowd and was the first to be gunned down. Although he was not a professional Soldier in an organized army, his bravery demonstrated that African Americans shared the same love for the newly founded America (Boston Massacre Historical Society, 2008).

When the Revolutionary War began, recruiting was difficult for the local militias. White settlers and merchants had mixed feelings about rebelling against Britain in fear of economic loss. Many blacks filled the ranks in the North and served in a major battle such as The Battle of Bunker Hill. During the Revolutionary period, two African Americans named Peter Salem and Salem Poor were present in the ranks (Sanders, 2010). Salem Poor was a free African American who lived in a town called Andover. He joined the minutemen at Concord and took up arms against the British on the 19 of April in 1775. He was later credited for shooting British Lt.-Col. James Abercrombie in the Battle of Bunker Hill on the 17 of June 1775 (Sanders, 2010). Peter Salem was also a free African American from Framingham who fought at Concord on 19 April. One week later, he joined the Sixth Massachusetts Regiment and fought alongside White Soldiers at Bunker Hill, killing British Major John Pitcairn (Sanders, 2010). These men demonstrated their willingness to fight for freedom and country, putting their challenges with racism aside.

In 1776, General George Washington lifted the ban on African Americans serving in the Continental Army that was voted in by the Continental Congress just one year prior. This allowed free Blacks to serve and receive compensation and the benefits just like the White Soldiers (Selig). Many states in the south continued to make laws against arming African Americans for fear of revolt. By 1777, Washington opened up more opportunities for African Soldiers. They were allowed to become artillery men, miners, and learn a skilled craft such as blacksmith, farrier, and wheelwright (Selig). Despite the difficulties, African Americans were willing to serve because they saw it as a freedom and a way to gain membership in the nation as citizens and not property. Blacks remained enslaved after the brave displays of loyalty.

Black's service in the military continued through the War of 1812 and into the Civil War, where Blacks served on both sides. Many still served in the same duties as the ones in the American Revolution, but they were also allowed to pick up arms. President Abraham Lincoln struggled with the idea of removing the ban on Blacks. He hesitated to authorize the Union Army to recruit African Americans into its ranks (U.S. Government, 2013). By the middle of 1862, however, the escalating number of escaped slaves and low numbers of white volunteers made it difficult to fill the ranks of the Union Army. Government officials began to consider lifting the ban on blacks in the military (U.S. Government, 2013). Volunteers began to enlist after Black leaders such as Frederick Douglass began encouraging Black men to become Soldiers. He saw this as a step toward full citizenship for Blacks as a whole. In May 1863, the Bureau of Colored Troops was established to accommodate the incredible amount of Black Soldiers that answered the call to duty. Statistics showed, "that by the end of the Civil War, roughly 179,000 black men (10% of the Union Army) served as Soldiers in the U.S. Army, and another 19,000 served in the Navy" (U.S. Government, 2013). Black units were not used in combat as extensively as they might have been because they were still not seen as equals. They were initially paid only ten dollars per month with a three dollar deduction for clothing. So they only brought home seven dollars in contrast to White Soldiers, who received thirteen dollars per month with no clothing deduction. Black Soldiers were finally granted equal pay in June 1864 by Congress and began to receive the same rations, supplies, and medical care as White Soldiers (U.S. Government, 2013). Over the course of the war, 16 Black soldiers earned the Medal of Honor for their valor. Two of the most notable male African American Civil War heroes were Sergeant William Carney and Captain Andre Cailloux.

William Harvey Carney was born in Norfolk, Virginia and enslaved in 1840. His father William Carney Sr. escaped slavery, began working, and eventually earned enough money to buy the freedom of his wife and son. Once he bought their freedom, they moved to New Bedford, Massachusetts. Growing up William Carney Jr. pursued training in ministry with the intent of becoming a preacher (Helm, 2005). His plans changed following the issuing of the Emancipation Proclamation. Instead of following his childhood dreams to preach, he decided to join in the Union army in 1863. After President Lincoln officially authorized the recruitment of Black Soldiers, Carney joined the 54th Massachusetts Black Infantry Regiment (Helm, 2005). Carney quickly made the rank of sergeant because of his education and his ability to lead others. The 54th was commanded by Colonel Robert Gould Shaw, who initially thought an all-Black regiment would defect and declined the offer. He reconsidered and took command only to discover that the free Blacks that made up his unit were very dedicated Soldiers, who impressed him even more over time.

During the summer of 1863, Shaw volunteered the 54th to lead an assault against a heavily fortified Confederate Fort. Shaw led the 54th in the assault on Fort Wagner but was killed alongside his flag bearer. Carney quickly took charge of the troops, seized the flag, and continued the assault until reinforcements arrived. Despite being wounded in the leg, Carney kept the flag waving as a symbol for the troops to rally around. After struggling back to the Union lines, Carney collapsed and shouted, "Boys the old flag never touched the ground" (Helm, 2005).

Carney was discharged from the infantry because of the wounds he suffered in the battle. Carney was awarded the Congressional Medal of Honor for his heroic acts at Fort Wagner. He was the first African American to receive our country's highest military award (Helm, 2005). The Massachusetts State House flew its flag at half-mast in his remembrance after his death in 1908. This was an honor usually given to a deceased governor, senator, congressman, or U.S. President (Helm, 2005).

Andre Cailloux was born a slave on a plantation in Plaquemines Parish, Louisiana. (African American Registry, 2013) When he was 5, his master died. Cailloux's family became the property of his master's widow, who moved him and his parents to New Orleans. He was trained in the craft of cigar making as a youth and worked at the local factory where he also learned to read. It was common to have a storyteller read to workers as they rolled cigars (African American Registry, 2013). At the age of 21, Cailloux gained his freedom and married Felicie Coulon, also a recently freed slave. They soon had children and became landowners. In 1860, they opened a small business in a neighboring town. Active in the social life of the Black Creole community, he was a well-liked, good-looking man who was trusted by others (African American Registry, 2013). He was an avid boxer and horseman, but he was best known for his manners and his character (African American Registry, 2013). He took pride in calling himself "the blackest man in New Orleans" (African American Registry, 2013).

Cailloux joined the Friends of Order, a Creole organization, and was quickly elected to an officer position. When the Civil War began the Colored often served under the governing power, which was the Confederacy at that time. He organized a unit with 100 members from the Friends of Order. It became the Order Company in the Louisiana Native Guards and included runaway slaves and free black men (African American Registry, 2013). The Confederates were cautious of the Black troops and because it was still a slave society, they lived with the constant fear of the slaves revolting. The Native guards were disbanded after the Union seized the city of New Orleans in May of 1862.

The Union recruited the Order Company and renamed it the Colored Company under the 1st Regiment. The capture of New Orleans in most people's minds signaled a significant turning point in the Civil War. It showed that Blacks were active participants in their own liberation and that one day they could defeat the slaveholders.

On May 27, 1863, General Nathaniel P. Banks initiated a poorly planned attack on a well-defended Confederate position called Port Hudson (African American Registry, 2013). Cailloux and over 100 men were ordered to lead an almost suicidal assault against the Confederate troops in the fortified Port. Cailloux's company suffered heavy casualties, but Cailloux continued shouting encouraging words to his men in French and English. On his Command they continued to advance and assault the enemy lines (African American Registry, 2013). On his last charge, he was shot in the arm. With it dangling by his side, Cailloux continued to lead the charge until he was killed by a Confederate artillery shell (African American Registry, 2013).

Cailloux became the first Black Officer in the Union Army to be killed in combat during the Civil War. He died heroically in the poorly planned attack on Port Hudson, Louisiana (African American Registry, 2013). Cailloux's heroism became a rallying cry for the recruitment of African Americans into the Union Army (African American Registry, 2013).

There were many African Americans that lost their lives on both sides during the Civil War. Black men took the opportunity to become leaders even in the harsh combat conditions. This leadership and the enlistment of Blacks in the military continued throughout history. World War II bore many African American leaders that still had to endure the enemy and racism. None is more interesting than the father/son legacy of Benjamin O. Davis Sr. and Benjamin O. Davis Jr.

Benjamin O. Davis Sr. was the first African American Army General Officer in the U.S. Armed Forces (U.S. Army Center of Military History, 2011). He was born in Washington, D.C. in 1877. He attended M Street High, an all-Black high school, which is where he received his first military training (Black Heritage Commemorative Society, 2011). He went on to attend Howard University where he joined the Eighth U.S. Volunteer Infantry. It was his experience in the volunteer force that prompted him to pursue a military career. He attempted to enroll in West Point but was denied because Blacks still lacked equal rights, so he had to enlist and work his way up to a commission (Black Heritage Commemorative Society, 2011).

Davis Sr. enlisted in the Army in June 1899 as a private in a Calvary unit. By 1900, he reached the rank of Squadron Sergeant Major and on February 2, 1901, he was commissioned a Second Lieutenant of Cavalry in the Regular Army. His assignments carried him around the world with his first being in the Philippines (U.S. Army Center of Military History, 2011). He moved around more than most because his superiors did not want him commanding White Soldiers or mixing with White Officers. He received assignments on the Mexican border and in Monrovia, Liberia (U.S. Army Center of Military History, 2011).

His progression through the ranks was somewhat abnormal compared to modern Army standards. He was promoted to; First Lieutenant on March 30, 1905; to Captain on December 24, 1915; to Major (temporary) on August 5, 1917; and to

Lieutenant Colonel (temporary) on May 1, 1918. He reverted to his permanent rank of Captain on October 14, 1919, and was promoted to Lieutenant Colonel on July 1, 1920; to colonel on February 18, 1930; to Brigadier General (temporary) on October 25, 1940. He was retired on July 31, 1941 and recalled to active duty with the rank of brigadier general the following day. (U.S. Army Center of Military History, 2011)

Davis was assigned again in 1931 to serve as Professor of Military Science and Tactics at Tuskegee until August 1937, when he was transferred to Wilberforce University (U.S. Army Center of Military History, 2011). In June of 1941, he was assigned Assistant Inspector General, a position he would hold again in 1946. In September of 1942, Davis was assigned to the European Theater of Operations. He was given a special duty as the Advisor on Negro problems. In November 1944, he became the Special Assistant to the Commanding General, Communications Zone in the European Theater of Operations and was stationed in Paris, France until 1945 (U.S. Army Center of Military History, 2011). He returned to his Assistant Inspector General position and retired in 1948, after 50 years of service.

Benjamin O. Davis Jr. inherited his father's leadership abilities and bravery. He was born in 1912, and as early as 13 years of age he was fascinated with flying. He attended a flying exhibition on Bolling Air Force Base where he experienced his first flight. One of the pilots allowed him to ride in his plane during the exhibition. That flight started Davis's drive to become a pilot himself (Burton, 2012).

While attending the University of Chicago in 1932, Davis solicited the help of Illinois Representative Oscar De Priest (the first Black Alderman in Chicago, and the only Black serving in Congress in 1932) to assist him in becoming a military pilot. De Priest sponsored him for a spot in the United States Military Academy in West Point, New

York (Burton, 2012). His time in the Academy was harsh, hostile, and relentless in the challenges and obstacles it put in his way. He spent four years of training and during that time none of his classmates would speak to him outside of the professional environment. None would be his roommate, nor sit with him to eat. Nonetheless, he graduated in 1936, finishing 35th in his class of 278 (Burton, 2012). When he received his commission as a Second Lieutenant in the Infantry, he became one of only two Black combat officers in the United States Army with the other being his father Benjamin O. Davis Sr. (Burton, 2012).

He applied for the Army Air Corp but was rejected because they did not have a Black squadron, so Davis was sent to an all-Black division located in Fort Benning, Georgia. He was not permitted to enter the Officer's club on the base even though he was a commissioned Officer (Burton, 2012). After graduating from the U.S. Army Infantry School, he was assigned to Tuskegee, Alabama to teach a military tactics course at the Tuskegee Institute just as his father was (Burton, 2012). In June of 1939, he was promoted to the rank of First Lieutenant and in later years became a Captain, then Major, and was temporarily promoted to Lieutenant Colonel (Burton, 2012).

Despite the assignment, he still wanted to fly along with other Blacks. Pressure was placed on the Roosevelt administration to allow Blacks into more combat roles at the beginning of World War II. As a result, President Roosevelt ordered the War Department to create a Black flying unit. Davis was assigned to the first class of colored servicemen at the Tuskegee Army Air Field (Burton, 2012). In 1942 he finished his training and was one of only five Blacks to complete the course and then became the first Black Officer to make a solo flight in an Army Air Corps plane (Burton, 2012). He was permanently promoted to the rank of Lieutenant Colonel and in July 1942 he was assigned as the commander of the 99th

Pursuit Squadron, known in history as the Tuskegee Airmen.

In 1943, the 99th Pursuit Squadron was assigned first to Tunisia, then to a combat mission in the German-held Island of Pantelleria and finally took part in the allied invasion of Sicily. In September, Davis was recalled to Tuskegee to take over a larger all-black unit preparing for combat in Europe, the 332nd Fighter Group (Burton, 2012). In 1944 Colonel Davis and the 332nd Fighter Group arrived in Italy, where they were based at Ramitelli Airfield. The 332nd, called the Red Tails because of the distinctive paint scheme on the tails of their planes, performed well as bomber escorts, often being requested by bomber pilots because of their insistence on not abandoning the bombers (Burton, 2012). The Tuskegee Airmen never lost a bomber, despite an onslaught of the latest and fastest enemy German planes. The 332nd won a Distinguished Unit Citation for the mission (National Park Service, 2000).

After the end of World War II, the new President Harry Truman dispatched an order to fully integrate the military branches. Colonel Davis was called upon to help draft the new "Air Force" plan for carrying out this order. His assignments took him from Europe to the Pentagon. When the Korean War broke out, he once again participated in the fighting, manning an F-86 fighter jet and leading the 51st Fighter-Interceptor Wing.

In the summer of 1949, Davis was assigned to attend the Air War College. He became the first African American to attend the college. Graduating from War College was significant because his future promotions depended on it. Although racism plagued Montgomery, Alabama, where the War College was located, he graduated and was assigned to serve in the United States Air Force Headquarters at the Pentagon. Davis Jr.'s assignments throughout the Air Force helped him achieve the rank of Brigadier General in

1960, Major General in 1962, and Lieutenant General in 1965. He retired after 33 years of military service in 1970.

President Bill Clinton pinned Davis with his fourth star in 1998, and stated: "General Davis is here today as living proof that a person can overcome adversity and discrimination, achieve great things, turn skeptics into believers; and through example and perseverance, one person can bring truly extraordinary change" (Burton, 2012). There have been several great African American Military leaders emerge since the Davis legacy broke down the walls, but none better known today than Colin Powell.

Colin Powell was born in 1937 in Harlem, New York. He was the son of Jamaican immigrants Luther and Maud Powell. Colin was raised in the South Bronx and graduated from Morris High School in 1954 (Colin Powell, 2013). Powell studied geology at City College of New York, where his passion for the military began. He joined the Reserve Officer Training Corp (ROTC) and soon became the commander of his unit. It was then that he determined a military career would give him structure and direction in his life (Colin Powell, 2013). Powell was commissioned as a Second Lieutenant in the U.S. Army in 1958. He was stationed in Fort Devens, Massachusetts where he met his wife, Alma Johnson and began a family in 1962 (Colin Powell, 2013).

In 1962, Powell went to South Vietnam as a military advisor and was wounded by a mine in a booby trap. In 1968 he returned as a Battalion Executive Officer for a second tour of duty. Powell earned two Purple Hearts, a Bronze Star, a Soldier's Medal, and the Legion of Merit for his service in Vietnam (John Patrick Sheehan, 2013).

Powell returned after his second tour and received his MBA from George Washington University in 1971. Shortly after his graduation he began a White House Fellowship which started his involvement in politics. He served as the executive assistant to the Secretary of Energy during the Carter administration and military assistant to the Defense Secretary during the Reagan administration (John Patrick Sheehan, 2013). He continued to advance his military career while he worked in the high-profile positions.

Powell served from 1987 to 1989 as President Ronald Reagan's national security advisor (John Patrick Sheehan, 2013). In 1989, under the Bush administration, he was made a four-star general and was appointed Chairman of the Joint Chiefs of Staff, becoming the youngest person and first African American to hold the post, achieving international prominence for his role in the U.S. military effort against Iraq (Operations Desert Shield and Desert Storm) in 1990 and 1991. He retired from the United States Army on September 30, 1993 (John Patrick Sheehan, 2013).

General Powell had an outstanding military career that later propelled him into the full-time political arena. In 2000, President George W. Bush appointed Colin Powell Secretary of State. He was the highest ranking African American during that time and was unanimously confirmed by the U.S. Senate (Colin Powell, 2013).

Since his retirement, Powell has remained vocal on political topics, openly speaking on a number of issues he recognized when in he was in office. In 2008, Colin Powell, known for his ties to the Republican Party, made headlines when he announced his endorsement of Barack Obama as his choice for President of the United States. Colin Powell came from average living conditions and became one of the most decorated African American Military leaders of all time.

Census reports from 2010 show that there are more than 2.4 million African American military veterans living in the United States. Current statistics show that the number of Americans enlisting declined significantly in all three military branches from 2000 through 2004 (Government, 2013).

It has decreased by 15% in the Army, 23% in the Marines and 11% in the Air Force (Government, 2013). The Navy has also reported declining numbers, but has remained about the same overall, unlike the other three branches (Government, 2013).

According to a Pentagon analysis conducted in response to questions from USA TODAY, "the primary reason for the trend is a sharp drop in Blacks joining the military" (Moniz, 2008). From 2000 to 2004, African American recruits in all four services fell by nearly a third, from 38,034 to 26,170. Several factors contributed to the decline. There has been a rise in Black college attendance, and the War in Iraq is not popular among Blacks (Moniz, 2008). The tremendous decline in Black Army recruits is due partly to a good news report. It shows that African Americans now have better career options outside the military (Moniz, 2008).

Freed Black men up to present day Warriors with thoughts of becoming included as part of the American dream put their lives on the line to defend America, some making the ultimate sacrifice after years of defending soil they once were not able to call their own.

CHAPTER V

• • •

Corporate Leaders

Captured African slaves arrived in America with just the skills they learned in their native land. Those skills helped build America into what it is today. Almost immediately they began to seek not only freedom, but they also began to seek enterprise. Free and enslaved alike, Black men have demonstrated the ability to start and manage their own businesses as early as the colonial days. Blacks that gained success in various businesses often created employment opportunities for other Blacks. Many of those businessmen also invested in the Black communities to help improve the quality of life for African Americans. This reinvestment in the community helped to create a Black middle class. Blacks began to emerge and prosper in sectors where whites shunned contact with blacks. This group included doctors, lawyers, undertakers, beauticians and barbers. Almost immediately, these individuals began

to pool their money to create larger independent businesses, support philanthropic organizations, and fund educational institutions (State Group LLC, 2013). Some of these
Black entrepreneurs stood out among the rest and paved
the way for the Black businessmen of today. This chapter
has an overview of some of those success stories beginning
with those of William Whipper and William Leidesdorf.

William Whipper was one of the wealthiest Americans of his time. He was born in Lancaster, PA in 1804.
Whipper was the mixed son of a White Pennsylvania businessman and a Black woman who was his servant (Sanders, 2010). After his father died, he inherited his successful
lumber business. With the help of his free Black business
partner, Stephen Smith, he created one of the state's leading lumberyards. Whipper made a sizable fortune from
the lumberyard and other joint ventures, which included
land holdings in Pennsylvania and Canada, railroad cars,
and a steam ship on Lake Erie (African American Registry, 2013). Many of these assets were directly employed
in aiding the escapes of Black fugitives from the South.

Whipper came to believe that White prejudice against
Black Americans was not from the color of their skin, but from
their condition. He later recanted that statement, but prior
to his change of heart he developed an idea known as "moral
reform." He sought to change the temperament of Blacks in
order for them to gain acceptance in the dominant White
American society (African American Registry, 2013). For
several decades, William Whipper operated an active station
of the Underground Railroad in Columbia. His contributions to antislavery are just as noteworthy as is his profitable
lumber business. Whipper was dedicated to nonviolence and
rational persuasion, helping to found the anti-slavery American Moral Reform Society (Sanders, 2010). William Whipper died in 1885 after years of serving as a model for other free

Blacks (African American Registry, 2013). In the same era emerged another entrepreneur named William Liedesdorf.

William Leidesdorf was born in 1810 in the Virgin Islands. His father was Danish, and his mother was an enslaved African. When he was a young man, Leidesdorff was sent to New Orleans to work for his uncle's cotton business as a master of ships sailing between New York and New Orleans (Houghton Mifflin). While in Louisiana he became a wealthy cotton broker. Soon afterward, both his father and uncle died, leaving him a good–sized inheritance (Houghton Mifflin).

In 1841, he bought a trading ship and sailed to California. Leidesdorff landed in a small village called Yerba Buena. This village is now known as San Francisco, California. Leidesdorff and his ship made regular trips between California and Hawaii to move materials and products between the two locations. He built a store, a warehouse, and a hotel on land grants from the Mexican government. Leidesdorff became a leader in the community. He bought a large house and hosted parties for visiting government officials, American and foreign alike (San Francisco African American Historical Society, 2013).

Leidesdorff died of brain fever in 1848 at the age of thirty-eight. He was recognized by his community for his contributions and was buried with the fullest honors any citizen could be rewarded. His name was not only credited with having the first hotel and warehouse, he also was America's first millionaire of African descent, and he was the first African American Diplomat serving as the U.S. Consul to Mexico (San Francisco African American Historical Society, 2013). More and more successful Black businesses began to emerge throughout the United States, started by entrepreneurs such as Arthur Gaston and John Johnson.

Arthur G. Gaston was born in Demopolis, Alabama in 1893. His father was a railroad worker, and his mother was a cook for a wealthy white family. His family moved to Birmingham, Alabama when he was a teenager. There his mother was employed by a wealthy Jewish department store owner named A. B. Loveman (Beito, 2006).

Loveman became Gaston's model of what success should be. He noticed that Loveman spent long hours working and investing wisely in his future. Although most of Gaston's wealth came from trial and error and luck, he followed Loveman's example which motivated him to enroll into the Tuggle Institute (Beito, 2006). The Tuggle Institute was modeled after Tuskegee University and taught industrial skills for trades and business. The school mirrored Tuskegee to such an extent that the headmaster, Booker T. Washington, would often visit Tuggle to deliver powerful motivational speeches (Beito, 2006). Gaston was blown away by Washington and began to follow his teachings. The first book he ever purchased was Washington's autobiography "Up From Slavery." Gaston's favorite passage read:

Every persecuted individual and race should get much consolation out of the great human law, which is universal and eternal, that merit, no matter under what skin found, is in the long run recognized and rewarded.... [T]he Negro ... should make himself, through skill, intelligence, and character, of such undeniable value to the community in which he lived that the community could not dispense with his presence. (Beito, 2006)

Gaston's wealthy role model and education did not grant him instant success. He watched closely as other black businessmen failed before going to serve in World War I. He returned home from war and took a job delivering dry cleaning, which did not pay much (Beito, 2006). Decent employment for Blacks was hard to find after the war, so in 1920 Gaston moved his mother to Westfield, Alabama and began working for the Tennessee Coal and Iron Company. His rent and other miscellaneous living expenses were deducted directly from his pay. Just like many other Blacks in the area, family was few and far apart. He began sharing his lunch that his mother prepared for him with men who had no one to cook for them (Jenkins).

Full of despair and ill from the paint fumes, Gaston began to think he would spend his life as a laborer in a mine. While Gaston was still faint from the fumes a coworker approached him about his lunch. He shared as always, but at that moment he realized that those men would pay for home cooked meals. With his mother at home cooking, Gaston began to sell box lunches, peanuts and popcorn to his coworkers (Jenkins).

He was so successful at running his food service he was able to save the money he earned at the mine. He was doing so well that he started a payday loan business. He loaned workers money until they received their pay checks and then collected the debt plus interest at twenty-five cents on the dollar (Jenkins). Gaston felt no guilt because he never fit in with the others since he did not squander his money away on things he did not need. Coworkers and even women shunned Gaston because most of the men that took out loans were trying to impress the ladies. He kept saving and curbed all spending habits while he looked for more business ventures (Jenkins).

Gaston was making money, but it was still necessary for him to work. He began searching for a business that would be long term and self-sustaining. He had a breakthrough when he stopped trying to figure out what he could sell. He took a look at his surrounding community and asked himself what it needed. This turn away from self-interest and toward public service, changed his business ventures for the rest of his life (Jenkins).

Gaston began selling burial insurance in his community, answering a call he had heard too many times. Around the mines, laborers would often collect money to people bury their loved ones. Funerals were becoming more and more expensive when ministers began to emphasize the importance of the deceased receiving their last rites. He believed that Blacks needed a way to take care of burying their own and not fall victim to increasing burial costs (Jenkins).

So in 1932, Gaston started the Booker T. Washington Burial Society. He started by collecting premiums door to door. It grew into one of the largest Black owned insurance companies in Alabama (Jenkins). Today, the Booker T. Washington Insurance Company has more than $54 million in assets. Because of this success Gaston was able to reinvest into other venues. He opened the Booker T. Washington College in 1939, the Citizens Federal Savings Bank in 1957, and Gaston Construction in 1980, to name a few.

During the Civil Rights Era, Gaston made his contributions behind the scenes. Even though his businesses were plagued by bomb threats, he put up bail money for jailed activists and even Martin Luther King Jr. himself (Press, 1968). His wealth in Alabama continued to attract trouble even into the late 1970s. Gaston was kidnapped in 1976 and held hostage in his own Cadillac. It was not until police stopped the suspicious looking driver that they found him beaten and bound with a bag over his head (Press, 1968). He remained active and carried on his day to day business even after suffering a stroke at 100 years of age in 1992. He passed away in 1996, leaving an empire worth nearly 130 million dollars. This is a true rags to riches story about a Black man who answered the call of his community. These success stories continued not only in the South but moved North as Blacks sought better education and better employment opportunities. One such success story is that of John H. Johnson, a product of a single parent home.

John H. Johnson was born in Arkansas City, Arkansas in 1918. His father was killed in a sawmill accident. Johnson's mother worked as a cook for the crews building levees along the Arkansas River. Desperate for her son to have a quality education and a better chance at life, she saved her money to buy a one-way ticket to Chicago (Brennan, 2005). Once they arrived in Chicago his mother enrolled him in the DuSable high school for Blacks. The school was known for the advanced academic programs it provided for its students (Brennan, 2005). He became the editor of the school newspaper and was elected class president before he graduated in 1936. The school newspaper was his introduction to mass media.

Johnson and other honor students were asked to speak at an urban league civil rights gathering. His presentation was so impressive the president of the Supreme Liberty Life Insurance Company offered him not only a job but also a scholarship for college (Brennan, 2005). He began working for the insurance company as their magazine editor and enrolled in Chicago University. While working for the insurance company he decided to start his own publication. He followed the Reader's Digest model, which was republishing condensed versions of existing publications (Brennan, 2005).

He applied for loans but was denied until he offered his mother's furniture as collateral for 500 dollars. He then sent out subscription offers to the policyholders of the Supreme Liberty Life Insurance Company (Brennan, 2005). He received over 3,000 subscriptions for his paper known as the Negro Digest. By November of 1942, he had over 50,000 subscribers.

His second publication was based on the Life magazine model. Johnson wanted to show society that Blacks were successful, had grand ceremonies, and enjoyed the same luxuries in life as most Whites (Brennan, 2005). He named the magazine Ebony and sold over 25,000 copies on its first publication in 1945. He began to revolutionize the magazine industry. He sold advertisement to retailers by convincing them to address the African American market. One of his first retailers was Zenith, followed by others which gave him credit for inventing a Black consumer's market (Brennan, 2005).

Johnson publishing company was going strong with the assistance of friends and family. Newsstands were reluctant to stock his magazines until Blacks began demanding them around Chicago, so Johnson asked 30 of his friends and family to go around the city purchasing and demanding his publications (Entrepreneur Media Inc, 2008). The ploy worked not only in Chicago, but Detroit, New York, and Philadelphia. Johnson's sales rose to more than 50,000 copies of Negro Digest a year.

In 1950, Johnson stopped the publication of Negro Digest and waited nearly 10 years to revive it as Black World (Entrepreneur Media Inc., 2008). In 1972 he began publishing a pocket size magazine called Jet. After he created Jet magazine, he expanded his company to include book publishing, a review club, and a Black make-up line. He became the first Black to own a broadcasting network after he purchased two radio stations in Chicago (Entrepreneur Media Inc, 2008).

Johnson's drive and determination has made him one of the wealthiest Black males in America. He has built the Johnson Publishing Company into the largest Black owned publisher in the world. When he was asked about his key to success, he stated;

There is no secret to success. You have to have a bit of luck, and you have to be at the right place at the right time. I was fortunate enough to have a mother who taught me very fundamental things about success. She taught me that you have to earn success, which means you have to prepare yourself, you have to work hard, you have to have commitment, and you have to have faith. You have to believe that things are possible. If there is a secret, the secret is in all those things. (Entrepreneur Media Inc., 2008)

Johnson continues to meet a demand that Black people had in the Chicago community just as Arthur G. Gaston did in Georgia. His empire continues to grow today.

These entrepreneurs have proven that African American men can build empires. Corporate America was somewhat of a challenge for Blacks. This challenge stemmed from the education system. Wealthy Whites were taught and trained to run companies in Business Colleges, whereas Blacks were taught technical skills in trade schools. Over time, education, persistence, and opportunities allowed Blacks to successfully climb the corporate ladder in some of America's largest companies. Two of those well-known corporate executives are Kenneth I. Chenault and Clarence Otis Jr.

Kenneth I. Chenault was born in 1951, in Mineola, New York (Bio.com, 2013). His parents were dentists and sent him to the Waldorf School in the Hempstead, New York. He excelled and served as class president of his senior year. The school focuses on developing students to be morally responsible and have individuals emerge with a high degree of social competence. He went on to graduate from Bowdoin College in 1973 and earn a Law degree from Harvard University in 1976 (UCLA).

After graduating Harvard, he worked for the Roger and Wells Law firm in New York for five years. In 1979 he landed a consulting job with Bain and Company where he stayed until he joined American Express in 1981. He worked his way to the top by assuming roles of more responsibility which gained him more recognition over the years. His track to success is as follows:

Chenault joined the company in September 1981 as Director of Strategic Planning. He was named President of the Consumer Card Group in 1989, and in 1993 he became President of Travel Related Services (TRS), which encompassed all of American Express's card and travel businesses in the United States. In 1995, he assumed additional responsibility for the company's worldwide card and travel businesses and also was named Vice Chairman

of American Express. Mr. Chenault became President
and Chief Operating Officer in February 1997. He assumed his current responsibilities as CEO on January 1,
2001, and as Chairman on April 23 of that year. (UCLA)

Chenault serves on several boards leading the way in public service. To name a few:

American Express, IBM, the Arthur Ashe Institute for
Urban Health, the National Center on Addiction & Sub-
stance Abuse at Columbia University, the Smithsonian
Institution's Advisory Council for the National Museum
of African American History & Culture, and the World
Trade Center Memorial Foundation (usa.gov, 2013).

He continues to serve as the CEO of American Express
and lives in New York with his wife Kathryn and two children.
His success started with a quality education, which led to opportunities that emerged from his persistent quest for success.

Clarence Otis Jr. was another great corporate executive
that came from some very discouraging living conditions and
rose to success. Otis Jr. was born in Vicksburg, Mississippi in
1956. His family moved to Los Angeles, California shortly afterwards. He grew up in Watts during the civil rights
movement of the 60's (NET Industries, 2013). His father
was a janitor, and his mother was a housewife. She pushed
the children to do their best in school. His father took them
for Sunday drives through Beverly Hills. Otis recalled in an
interview, "Those drives showed me how the other half lived,
and they made me believe another life was possible" (Horovitz, 2006). The boost from his mother helped him become a
high school standout, which led to a scholarship to Massachusetts' prestigious Williams College (NET Industries, 2013).

He graduated magna cum laude from Williams College in
1977. He went on to graduate from Stanford Law School on
1980. Otis worked in corporate laws thorough the 80's (NET
Industries, 2013). He specialized in mergers and acquisitions

and worked for some firms such as Donovan Leisure Newton & Irvine and Gordon, Hurwitz, Butowsky, Weitzen, Shalov & Wein. This exposed the young lawyer to the elite class of the rich and wealthy. He rubbed elbows with chief executives of major corporations (NET Industries, 2013).

He married Jacqueline Bradley in 1983 and became the board director of the Orlando Aviation Authority. Otis at the age of 30 became more fascinated by the financial side of business rather than the law side. He joined an investment firm named Kidder, Peabody, and Company, and by 1987 he was the vice president of the First Boston Corporation. His career has cast him into becoming one of the most powerful Black executives in America. His career track includes:

Serving as managing director of Giebert Municipal Capital in 1990 and 1991 and as Vice President and later Managing Director in Chemical Bank's (now JP Morgan) securities arm from 1991 to 1995. He played a key part in turning around the bank's struggling public finance division, shepherding funding of $2.6 billion for tax-exempt pollution-control projects, and he participated in a $208 million New York City bond issue that was named the deal of the year by Institutional Investor magazine. (NET Industries, 2013)

In 1995, Otis was recruited by Darden Restaurants to oversee their financial activities. He believed the company was on the rise (Black Entrepreneur Profile, 2013). His belief became reality, and he began to climb the corporate ladder becoming the Senior Vice President of Finance in 1997 and Chief Financial Officer in 1999. His vision and ability to manage the properties all over the country impressed his bosses. They named him President of the Smokey Bones restaurant division from 2002 to 2004 (Black Entrepreneur Profile, 2013). In 2004, he became Darden Restaurant's Chief Executive Officer and in 2005 he became the Chairman of the Board. He also served as the Director of Verizon Communications.

Clarence Otis is one of only 4 African American Chief Executive Officers of America's Fortune 500. When Otis became the Chief Executive Officer of Darden Restaurants in December of 2004, there were seven Black "Fortune 500" CEO's. He credits the skills he learned in Watts for aiding in his success. He stated that, "growing up in Watts taught him something more important: how to size up all situations. That skill has literally taken him to the top of Corporate America's food chain" (Horovitz, 2006). He currently resides in Orlando, Florida with his wife, retired Senior Vice President of SunTrust Bank.

There have been only 13 Blacks that have risen to the ranks of Chief Executive Officer in Fortune 500 companies. Currently there are five Black men serving: Kenneth Frazier of Merck & Company, Roger Ferguson Jr. of TIAA-CREF, Kenneth Chenault of American Express, Don Thompson of McDonalds, and Clarence Otis Jr. of Darden Restaurants Inc.

Young Black entrepreneurs keep answering the call of the community by creating markets that the communities embrace. Black enterprise has expanded into the music industry, clothing, and products Black consumers prefer. One of the youngest success stories from these new enterprises is that of Sean John Combs.

Sean John Combs was born in Harlem in 1969 (Mars, 2012). He was raised in a single parent home by his mother Janice Combs. She modeled and raised Sean after his father was murdered in 1974. He attended a Catholic boy's school in the Bronx where he earned his nickname "Puffy" (Bio.com). He entered Howard University after he graduated high school but withdrew from college after Uptown Records hired him to be their Director of Talent. While he was at Howard, he was known for throwing dance parties and running a shuttle service to the airport. He also landed a dance position with MC Hammer.

His career in the music industry began when he began to sign talent such as Mary J. Blige to Uptown Records. This motivated Combs to branch out and create his own label called Bad Boy records in 1994 (Mars, 2012). At just 25 years of age he signed two artists initially, rappers by the name of Craig Mack and the Notorious B.I.G. He went on to sign artists such as New Edition, Lil Kim, and Aretha Franklin. Bad Boy Records grew to over 112 signees and is currently a joint venture with the Universal Music Group (Mars, 2012). In 1996 Combs sold 50% of his holdings to Universal.

After his friend Notorious B.I.G. was murdered in 1997, Combs released a single tribute song which lead to the launch of his first album called, "No Way Out" (Bio.com). Bad Boy Records sold more than 3.4 million copies of that album sold more than $100 million in recording that same year. In 1999, Combs launched his clothing line called, "Sean John" (Mars, 2012).

In 2003 Combs renegotiated the contract with the Universal Music Group and retained 100% ownership of Bad Boy Records. By 2004 the record label had very few releases until artists Brandy and Timberland breathed new life into a 2006 collaboration release called Press Play. The label now has annual sales over $100 million and is coupled with his Sean John clothing line (Mars, 2012). He also created cologne in a joint venture with Estee Lauder that became a best seller in department stores nationwide in 2005. In 2007 he signed a deal with Diageo to manage the sale and distribution of Ciroc Vodka, being a first in the liquor industry. The 50/50 split of the profit yields Combs nearly $100 million a year. In 2008, Combs acquired the Enyce clothing line from Liz Claiborne for $20 million and announced a new cable channel in 2012 called Revolt due to air in 2013. In April of 2012 Forbes estimated Sean "Puffy" Combs is worth more than $500 million and growing.

From slavery to now, Black men have sought economic worth in America. Black men have labored, toiled, educated themselves, pooled resources, and took unprecedented risks to become economic partners in America. Although initially the executive ranks were filled by Whites, Blacks continue to leap forward seeking more involvement in industry. Following the same visions that many had in the past, Black entrepreneurs continue to create new markets and answer the call of the Black community. They continue to actively seek positions in corporate America by meeting the educational requirements and gaining the experience it requires to take part in shaping the American economy.

CHAPTER VI

• • •

Government Leaders

America began to establish its government following the American Revolution and signing of the Declaration of Independence. The colonists' quest for liberty, equality, and justice for all motivated them to revolt against England. That longing for independence led them to develop the American Constitution and establish a democratic government. After the Constitution was ratified in 1789, the three branches of government and a system of checks and balances became law and were accepted by all thirteen states in 1790. The American Constitution has been the longest standing governing document throughout the entire world. It established political offices such as the presidential, the congressional, and the gubernatorial. The Constitution also established the guidelines and the qualifications candidates must possess to gain a position in a government office. The Constitution also gave African Americans and abolitionists the base for their argument that slavery was illegal, unconstitutional, and violated basic human rights. Prior to the Civil War, Blacks were considered property and had no rights as citizens. They could only ask for change by petitioning the courts and formally addressing the nation's political leaders. Free Blacks in the Northern States knew that true equality required African Americans to be involved in government. Orators and educators such as Frederick Douglass and W.E.B. DuBois urged Blacks to get involved. Blacks became involved in local and state level governments as early as 1836, despite not being allowed to vote or hold an office in the federal government. This chapter will give an overview of some African Americans who have held positions in the government from 1836 to now. One of the first Blacks elected to a political office was Alexander Twilight.

Alexander Twilight was born in Corinth, Vermont in 1795 (Winter, 2011). His parents were fair skinned or mixed-race Blacks named Ichabod and Mary Twilight. The town records show them to be the first Blacks to settle in Corinth (Orleans County Historical Society, 2013). The historical society believed Twilight's parents to be freed slaves and the product of racially mixed unions. Ichabod reportedly served as a private in the Continental Army during the American Revolution.

Twilight began working on a neighboring farm at just eight years of age (Winter, 2011). He learned reading, writing, and arithmetic as a youth laboring on the farm. He saved enough money to enroll in Randolph's Orange County Grammar School at the age of twenty in 1815. He completed high school and two years of college by 1821 (Orleans County Historical Society, 2013). He applied to Middleburg College after his graduation and was accepted. He enrolled as a junior and was the first Black to earn a bachelor's degree from an American University.

Twilight moved to Peru, New York and began teaching from 1824 to 1828 (Orleans County Historical Society, 2013). While living in Peru, Twilight met his wife, Mercy Ladd Merrill, studied theology, and became a licensed minister in Plattsburgh by 1826. In 1829, Twilight relocated to Brownington and accepted not only a position as the school principal but also the Brownington Congregational Church, which ordained him their pastor in the same year (Orleans County Historical Society, 2013). He resigned his position as pastor in 1834 to pursue building a four-story grammar school complete with dorm rooms, a kitchen, a dining room, six recital rooms, and two large classrooms. He completed his project in 1836 and called it Athenian Hall (Orleans County Historical Society, 2013).

That same year Twilight was elected as a representative by his community. He was sent to the Vermont state legislature in October of 1836 to argue that the counties should not allow his county's schools to split into two schools. He believed, "that if the County's resources for education were to be split two ways, there could follow more schools which would become increasingly mediocre" (Orleans County Historical Society, 2013). He was the first Black elected to a political position at a state level in the United States. In 1847, Twilight moved to Quebec for five years but later returned to Brownington to serve as its school headmaster. He died in 1857, and his Athenian Hall has been converted into the Orleans County Society Museum (Winter, 2011).

Race discrimination and laws continued to limit the number of Blacks holding office until the 20th century. Numerous African American politicians made their mark on shaping American history and public policy after the Civil War such as Hiram Revels and Joseph Rainey.

Hiram Rhodes Revels was born in 1827 to a racially mixed couple in Fayetteville, North Carolina. His father was a Baptist minister, and his mother was of Scottish descent (Clarity Digital Group LLC, 2012). He was taught to read and write by a free Black woman and at the age of eleven, Revels moved with his brother Elias to Lincolnton, North Carolina. Elias ran a barber shop that Revels inherited after his death in 1941. He left North Carolina to pursue ministry (Clarity Digital Group LLC, 2012). He enrolled in Indiana's Beech Grove Quaker Seminary and later transferred to a Black seminary in Ohio. He was ordained in 1845 by the African Methodist Episcopal Church. He began to minister throughout the 1850s in several states such as Illinois, Indiana, Tennessee, Missouri, and Maryland. He was jailed once for ministering to other Blacks in the state of Missouri in 1854 but was later released without incident (Clarity Digital Group LLC, 2012).

While he ministered in Maryland, Revels opened his own private school. In 1855, he left to continue his education after receiving a scholarship to Knox College in Galesburg, Illinois. He was one of the few Blacks to attend college during this period in history (Clarity Digital Group LLC, 2012).

In 1860, after the beginning of the Civil War, Revels recruited two Black regiments of Soldiers in Maryland (United States Congress, 2013). He served as a Chaplin to the African American troops in Mississippi where he also established churches. In 1863, after the war was over, he began to minister in Kansas, Kentucky, and Louisiana before he returned to Mississippi (United States Congress, 2013). In 1866, Revels settled in Natchez, Mississippi where he continued to minister. He also met his wife and began a family.

By 1868, Revels had opened several Black schools. His popularity thrust him into the local political arena. He was elected to an Alderman position in Natchez that same year. He was able to win support from Whites and Blacks but not without opposition (Clarity Digital Group LLC, 2012). In 1870, the Mississippi state Congress selected Revel to fill their seat in the United States Senate vacated by Jefferson Davis, who became the President of the Confederacy (Bio. com, 2013). Revels became the first African American to serve in the United States Senate, elected by a vote of 81 to 15 in the state of Mississippi (Clarity Digital Group LLC, 2012). John R Lynch, a Congressman from the 6th District stated:

So far as known, he [Revels] had never voted, had never attended a political meeting, and of course, had never made a political speech. But he was a colored man, and presumed to be a Republican, and believed to be a man of ability and considerably above the average in point of intelligence (Clarity Digital Group LLC, 2012).

He was also present when Revels delivered the opening prayer for the Mississippi state legislator and commented:

That prayer – one of the most impressive and eloquent prayers that had ever been delivered in the [Mississippi] Senate Chamber – made Revels a United States Senator. He made a profound impression upon all who heard him. It impressed those who heard it that Revels was not only a man of great natural ability, but that he was also a man of superior attainments. (Clarity Digital Group LLC, 2012)

Revels resigned from the Senate after a year to accept the Presidency of Alcorn Agricultural and Mechanical College, located in Claiborne County, Mississippi, which is now known as Alcorn State University until 1874. He retired from education in 1882 after teaching theology at Shaw University but continued his ministry until his death in 1901 (United States Congress, 2013).

Joseph Hayne Rainey was born in 1832 to Grace and Edward L. Rainey in Georgetown, South Carolina (United States Congress, 2013). His father was a barber who was allowed to cut hair as long as he shared the profits with his master. He earned enough to buy his family's freedom in the early 1840s. He later relocated to Charleston and began to barber at a luxury hotel named Mills House (United States House of Representatives, 2013). Even though his father had some success as a businessman Joseph only

received a limited education, so he took up the family trade (United States House of Representatives, 2013).

Rainey moved to Philadelphia and continued to barber.
He met his wife there and started a family. In 1861, the
Confederate Army called Rainey to dig trenches and build
fortifications. He later was assigned to a ship as a cook
and steward on a Confederate trade ship (United States
House of Representatives, 2013). In 1862, he escaped with
his wife to the West Indies until the end of the Civil War.

While in the Indies, Rainey ran his own barber shop, and
his wife opened a small dress shop. They saved their money
and returned to Charleston, South Carolina and were considered very wealthy in 1866. That wealth gave him influence
which thrust him into public service the very next year. He
served as the county chair for Georgetown, South Carolina
in 1877, the Georgetown Census taker in 1869, and in 1860,
he became an agent for the state land commissioner and a
Brigadier General in the State Militia. He was selected to
fill a vacant seat in the State Senate in 1870 after congressman Franklin Whittemore was removed for wrongdoing
(United States House of Representatives, 2013). That same
year Rainey was reelected for a full term becoming the first
Black to be elected to serve in the House of Representatives
(United States Congress, 2013). He continued to serve for
three full terms from 1870 to 1879 (United States Congress,
2013). He resigned and began a banking and brokerage
firm in Washington, retiring in 1886 at the age of 54. He
died one year later in 1887 (United States Congress, 2013).

Throughout the post-Civil War era and Reconstruction,
Blacks became more active in local, state, and federal governments. Barriers came down, and Blacks actively pursued
having a voice in the shaping of America. The passing of the
Thirteenth Amendment in 1865, the Fourteenth Amendment in 1868, and the Fifteenth Amendment in 1870 made

slavery illegal, granted freed Blacks citizenship, and guaranteed them the right to vote. These Amendments to the United States Constitution gave Blacks the same rights as Whites, but it took nearly one-hundred years and the Civil Rights Movement before they were enforced nationwide. Over 2,000 Blacks held office during the Reconstruction period, mostly at the local level (History.com, 2013). Angry White citizens turned to violence, intimidation, and even murder. At least 35 Black officials were murdered in the South during Reconstruction which ended in 1877 (History. com, 2013). The last Black elected to Congress during this era left office in 1901, and no other African American had served in Congress for nearly 28 years (Black Past, 2011). The years of intimidation helped spark the Civil Rights Movement and did not stop Blacks from seeking office. African American politicians such as Oscar DePreist continued to pursue having a voice in American government.

Oscar DePriest was born in Florence, Alabama in 1871 (United States Congress, 2013). His parents, both former slaves, moved to Salina, Kansas in 1878. He attended elementary school there and later enrolled in Salina's Normal school where he majored in bookkeeping. He earned a living by painting and decorating. In 1889, he moved to Chicago and entered into the real estate business. The Republican Party recruited him for his good work ethic and organizational skills (Chicago Tribune, 2013).

They nominated him to be the Cook County Commissioner in 1904, where he served until 1908. DePriest went on to become an Alderman for the city of Chicago from 1915-1917 but had to resign his position after being accused of accepting bribes. He was later acquitted of all charges, but the allegations and entire ordeal still damaged his reputation in the community (Bio.com, 2013). He returned to public office in 1924 when he joined Chicago's Third Ward Committee.

In 1928, DePriest was nominated by the Republican Party to fill a vacant seat in Congress. He won by a narrow margin and faced opposition from southern members of Congress who refused to work in offices located next to his. He was the first Black to hold an office in over 28 years. One of the most memorable moments during his terms was when his wife, Jessie, was invited to the White House for tea by First Lady Louise Hoover (Chicago Tribune, 2013). The invitation sent waves of discontent throughout the South. DePriest did not waver form his duties and was quoted saying, "I've been elected to Congress the same way as any other member. I'm going to have the rights of every other Congressman, no more, no less, if it's in the Congressional barber shop or at a White House tea" (Bio.com, 2013). He worked on several committees such as Indian Affairs, Post Office, Enrolled Bills, and the Post Roads Committees (Bio.com, 2013).

In 1933, he helped develop an antidiscrimination amendment during the establishment of the Civilian Conservation Corp (Civilian Conservation Corp, 2013). The Corp was established to promote environmental conservation but failed to allow Blacks any rolls in the heavily segregated South (Civilian Conservation Corp, 2013). By 1936, at least ten percent of the participants were Black. He left Congress the following year and returned to Chicago as an Alderman. He served in that position until 1947 and passed away in 1951 (United States Congress, 2013). Black men continued to be shunned throughout the Civil Rights Movement, where leaders such as Reverend Jessie Jackson, discussed in the previous chapter, emerged. Jackson ran twice unsuccessfully for the Office of the President of the United States in 1984 and 1988. During the unrest, Cleveland, Ohio elected its first African American Mayor named Carl Burton Stokes, which led to the election of Richard Hatcher in Gary, Indiana.

Carl Burton Stokes was born in Cleveland, Ohio in 1927. His father passed away when he was just three years old. His mother raised him alone in America's first federally funded housing project called Outhwaite Homes (Ohio History Central, 2013). His first challenge was overcoming the conditions he grew up in. Stokes dropped out of high school to work in a foundry in order to help support the family. His mother worked as a cleaning lady in the low economic area in order to support him and his younger brother Louis (USA Hero). Stokes joined the military in 1944. After serving two years in the United States Army, he returned to Cleveland to finish high school in 1947.

Stokes enrolled initially into West Virginia College. He then continued his studies at the Cleveland College of the Western Reserve and completed his Bachelor of Science degree in 1954 at the University of Minnesota Law School. He went on to acquire a Law Degree from the Cleveland-Marshall Law School in 1956 (Ohio History Central, 2013). Within one year of him passing the bar exam, Stokes was appointed to the position of Assistant Prosecutor for the city of Cleveland in 1958.

Stokes served in that position until 1962, when he joined his younger brother and opened their own law firm named Stokes, Stokes, Character, and Terry. He quickly got involved in politics and took an interest in the Civil Rights Movement (Ohio History Central, 2013). He was also elected to be a Representative in the Ohio House of Representatives. He was the first African American democrat to hold a position in the Ohio House and went on to serve three consecutive terms (Ohio History Central, 2013).

His political career did not end his quest to be a leader in the community. In 1965 Stokes entered the race for Mayor of Cleveland but lost. He ran again in 1967 and defeated the grandson of former President of the United States William

Taft named Seth Taft. He became the first African American Mayor of a major city. While in office, Stokes opened the door for other Blacks to enter the Cleveland city government. He was not without dark times and race riots, unexplained shootings and economic hardship plagued his years in office. The riots caused the White residents to flee to the suburbs, not only taking their money but also their businesses and jobs. In July of 1968, the streets erupted into a combat zone, or what is known today as the Glenville Shootout. The police engaged in a shootout with a Black neighborhood militant group that lasted for three days. It was reported that 7 people died and 15 were wounded by the time the shooting stopped (University of Cleveland). The event cast a dark shadow on the Stokes administration. He later wrote about the incident in his autobiography called, "Promises of Power." He was reelected to office in 1969 but did not run for a third term in 1971 (Ohio History Central, 2013).

Stokes walked away from politics and became New York's first African American television news anchor until 1980. He returned to his law practice representing the United Auto Workers Union until he became a Municipal Court Judge in 1983 (USA Hero). He served until he was appointed to be the United States Ambassador to Seychelles by the President William Clinton administration in 1984. While serving as Ambassador, he fell ill and was later diagnosed with throat cancer. Carl Burton Stokes died in 1996.

Stokes held three positions that had not previously been held by Blacks after overcoming the poor economic conditions of the Cleveland projects. His brother Louis went on to serve the public in several capacities following the trail he blazed. His personal sacrifice paid off with a very rewarding career, which opened the doors for more Blacks to enter into Ohio's government.

Richard Gordon Hatcher was born in 1933 in Michigan City, Indiana. His mother Catherine was a factory worker, and his father Carlton Hatcher worked for Pullman Railcar Manufacturing. He was the youngest of 13 children and blind in one eye (J Rank.org). His disability did not stop him from earning an athletic scholarship to Indiana University.

Hatcher completed his bachelor's degree in business and government in 1956, and a bachelor with honors in criminal law. He went on to earn his Juris Doctorate from Valparaiso University School of Law in 1959 (History Makers, 2012). Hatcher began his political career at Valparaiso University by participating in sit-ins and by working with the local National Association for the Advancement of Colored people.

After passing the bar, Hatcher started a private law practice in Gary, Indiana and quickly became the deputy county prosecutor in 1961. He ventured more into politics by running for Gary City Council. He won a seat in 1963 and became the first freshman elected to be the City Council President. He went on to become the first African American mayor of Gary, Indiana and the second to be elected Mayor of a major city. He took office just months after Carl Stokes was elected Mayor of Cleveland.

Hatcher served five terms, a span of twenty years. During his time in office, Hatcher was known for developing new approaches for urban problems and a being spokesman for civil rights, minorities, and the poor (History Makers, 2012). Just like Stokes, Hatcher had dark days in office. Gary fell into tough economic times, mainly because White City Officials refused to work with him initially, and White flight. At the time of his election Gary was one of the most segregated cities in the United States and was actually known as a sundowner town. Sundowners were towns where Blacks could move about freely during the day, but at sundown they were restricted to their neighborhoods or faced harassment. Also, a rapid decline in the steel industry cost the city jobs and his administration vital tax revenue (University of Washington, 2013). The city did manage to avoid the race riots that plagued many major cities during the 1960's. He did manage to promote Black business by awarding large contracts to Black entrepreneurs (University of Washington, 2013). He was defeated in the primaries during his sixth attempt to run for office in 1987.

After his defeat, Hatcher opened a consulting firm, Gordon Hatcher and Associates, and began teaching law at his alma mater, Valparaiso University in Valparaiso, Indiana in 1989 (University of Washington, 2013). Hatcher also served as Jessie Jackson's Campaign Chairman in 1984 and his advisor in the 1988 race for the Presidency of the United States. Hatcher ran again for mayor of Gary in 1991 but was defeated in the primary. Hatcher has written articles about urban affairs, civil rights, politics and law, and has been working on a book (Indiana Historical Society, 2013).

Blacks such as Stokes and Hatcher continued the quest for equality, and by the 1990's it became a common practice for voters to elect Blacks as Mayors in the large industrialized cities in the Northeast and Midwest (Biles, 1977). Cities that were predominantly Black and known as Sunbelt Cities such as Atlanta and Birmingham followed suit. Blacks have had more success in this area of politics than any other group, partly because of the continued White flight from urban areas (Biles, 1977). Doors continued to open in the 1990's, and America saw the election of its first African American Governor named Lawrence Douglas Wilder.

Lawrence Douglas Wilder was born in 1931 to Robert and Beulah wilder in Richmond Virginia. He was the grandson of slaves. His parents named him Douglas after Fredrick Douglass the great abolitionist and orator (Virginia Union University, 2013). They lived in the Church Hill District of

Richmond. He had six sisters and one brother. In 1951, he graduated from Virginia Union University with a degree in chemistry. He entered the Army after graduation and served during the Korean War. He earned a Bronze Star for his actions in combat (Virginia Union University, 2013).

He returned to Virginia and began working as a Chemist for the State Medical Examiner. He decided to study law, but Virginia's law schools had not been integrated and did not allow Blacks (Virginia Union University, 2013). He went on to graduate from Howard University Law School in 1959 (National Visionary Leadership Project). He returned to Richmond to open a firm named Wilder, Gregory and Associates, which was one of the few minority firms of this time.

He started his political career in 1969 and ran for a seat in Virginia's State Senate (National Visionary Leadership Project). He served five terms and sat on the transportation and the social services committees. He was the first African American elected to Virginia's Senate following Reconstruction. In 1985, he ran for the office of Lieutenant Governor and won, becoming the first African American to be elected in the United States (National Visionary Leadership Project). Wilder went on to become the first African American Governor elected to office in 1990. He was credited for balancing the state's budget and boosting Virginia to be recognized as one of the nation's best managed states (National Visionary Leadership Project). He served until 1994, continuing his active role as a public servant. He later became the Mayor of Richmond from 2005-2009 (Virginia Union University, 2013). Prior to him accepting his role as Mayor, he hosted a radio talk show, became an instructor at Virginia's Commonwealth University, and founded the National Slavery Museum in Fredericksburg, Virginia (National Visionary Leadership Project). There are many Black politicians, too numerous to mention, that held offices and carried the African American

Race to where we are today. The most accomplished African American elected into office is President Barack Obama.

President Barack Hussein Obama II was born in Hawaii in 1961 to Barack Obama Senior, a native of Kenya, and Ann Dunham of Kansas (The White House, 2013). His parents met while attending the University of Hawaii, married, and divorced in 1964. He met his father, who had become the Finance Minister of Kenya, only once in 1971. Obama Senior died in a car accident in 1982 (Barack Obama Biography, 2013). He was raised with the help of his grandparents. His mother went on to marry an Indonesian named Lolo Soetoro in 1967 and moved to Indonesia that same year (Barack Obama Biography, 2013). Obama returned to live with his grandparents in Hawaii after his fourth-grade year of elementary school. He remained in Hawaii until he graduated High School. He moved to Los Angeles California and began studying political science at Occidental College, which led to him enrolling in Columbia College of New York after just two years (Barack Obama Biography, 2013). He worked his way through college, won scholarships, and took out student loans to pay for his education (The White House, 2013).

He moved to Chicago in 1983 and began working as a community organizer with church based groups. His work in the community helped him realize that change would only come by changing the laws through politics (Keep and Share, 2013). This motivated Obama to apply for Harvard's Law School and complete his Juris Doctorate in 1991. While at Harvard, he became the first African American to be the President of the Harvard Law Review (Keep and Share, 2013). He returned to Chicago and began to practice law as a civil rights attorney. He also began to teach constitutional law at the University of Chicago Law School where he wrote a book on racial relations (The White House, 2013). The manuscript was published in 1995 and was called "Dreams of My Father." A few months later his mother died from cancer. During his years at Chicago University, he met his wife, Michelle Robinson.

Obama served on several boards in Chicago, such as board of directors of Chicago Annenberg Challenge, Chicago Lawyer's Committee for Civil Rights Law, the Centre for Neighborhood Technology, and Lugenia Burns Hope Center (Barack Obama Biography, 2013). He began organizing voter registration drives in 1992, which led to him running for a seat in the Illinois State Senate. The drive registered more than 150,000 African Americans and was the most successful in history (Barack Obama Biography, 2013).

After being elected to the State Senate in 1997, Obama worked for ethical and criminal justice reform. He helped pass laws that restricted the use of campaign funds, helped expand health care, passed law enforcement reform in Illinois, and created an income tax credit (Barack Obama Biography, 2013).

In 2002, Obama set his sights on the United States Senate. In 2004, he became the fifth African American to be elected to the Senate in history. While in office, he helped shape lobby reform, change gun laws, and bring transparency to federal spending (The White House, 2013). Obama joined several committees such as the Foreign Relations, the Environment and Public Works, and the Veteran's Affairs Senate committees (Barack Obama Biography, 2013). He also took on assignments serving on the Committees of Health, Education, Labor and Pension, Homeland Security, and Government Affairs (Barack Obama Biography, 2013). This led to him being nominated by the Democratic Party as their candidate for the 2008 race for Presidency. He was elected to the Office of the President of the United States in November of 2008 and served a second term after being re-elected in 2012.

From slavery to now, African Americans have representation in the highest office in America; however, the struggle

is far from over. It will take time for more African Americans to reach more local, state, and national offices. African Americans still struggle with the right to vote and bal-
looning campaign cost. Politics is still a challenging field
for Blacks that come from economically challenged areas.

CHAPTER VII

• • •

Conclusion

This book is an overview of great African American men and how they have fared as leaders from slavery to now. I focused on leaders in areas such as the educational field, the religious sector, corporate America, the United States military, and the United States government. Not only have Blacks overcome tremendous adversity just to become citizens of America, but they also have excelled in every area.

My research on the history of African American men has revealed the struggle and tremendous sacrifice they endured after being introduced as slaves to the new found America in the 1600s. Blacks emerged as citizens even after many White colonists shunned them, denied them freedom, and treated them as mere property. Colonists developed some patterns very early that grew from fear. The colonists were afraid of a slave revolt. That fear developed into racism and a prejudice based mostly on skin color. That prejudice has carried on for generations, even after the brutal Civil War. Hate groups such as the Klu Klux Klan continued to terrorize Blacks and any citizens that promote equality in America well after Blacks were set free.

Laws such as the Jim Crow laws created a separate but equal environment that took years to overcome. Dr. Martin Luther King Jr.'s non-violent approach to ending discrimination taught a world that everyone can flourish in America, whether White, Black, or Other.

Prior to Dr. King and the Civil Rights Movement, Blacks kept injecting themselves into society through various avenues. There were not many that went unopposed. The struggle from the beginning and even more so after the ratification of the 13th amendment has been for human rights, racial equality, and economic opportunities. I was able to comprise a list of successful African American men in each area who opened doors for other Blacks to follow in their quest for equality.

I began with scholars such as Richard Allen, born in 1760, who was one of the first to open schools for Blacks, and America's leading brain surgeon in 2013, Dr. Keith Black, who leads the world in preforming successful high risk surgeries. He also has developed new techniques and takes on the impossible cases. These gentlemen, along with countless others, demonstrated the value of an education. An education proved to be a valuable tool for African Americans. The struggle for the right to an education has benefited the world with the contributions being made by leaders such as Dr. Black.

Today, areas in the Southern United States still struggle with segregation issues. For example, Little Rock, Arkansas is still working to resolve school desegregation issues stemming from a federal ruling in the 1954 Brown vs. the Board of Education of Topeka, Kansas case. States such as Arkansas were refusing to integrate their public schools. On September 4, 1957, nine African American students attempted to enter Central High School in Little Rock,

Arkansas, but were prevented from entering by the Arkansas National Guard under the direction of the Governor of the State. The President of the United States responded by sending federal troops to escort the children to school and to prevent any incidents from happening. Currently, a hearing has been set for parties to work out a resolution to the forty-year-old business of desegregating Little Rock schools. So I find that struggle appears far from over in the educational arena. Despite the continued struggle, I found that more Black males are graduating from high school and entering college now more than ever. Statistics show that:

An increasing number of African American students are graduating high school. There is some confusion when only looking at the 4-year graduation rates, which show the Black graduation rate at only 63.6% compared to the U.S. graduation rate of 80.6%. But when looking at the dropout rate, one can see that only 8% of African American children dropped out of high school in 2010 compared to 7.4% of all children. This continues a long downward trend once at 21.3% in 1972, and 13.1% in 2000. African American high school seniors are planning to attend colleges and universities in increasing numbers and looking to technical schools and military service less since 1990. The number of Black seniors who had definite plans to attend a four-year college doubled from 1990 to 2010 from 30% to 60%. Those who had plans to go on to a graduate or professional school also doubled during the same time period. During the same time, plans to attend a two-year college only increased slightly from 16% to 19%. (U.S Department of Education, 2013)

Had the brave scholars of yesterday not pushed other African Americans to seek an education, the Black Race would not have advanced as far as it has today.

In the religious sector, African American slaves were taught Christianity by their owners. Men like Nat Turner used the vessel to start the largest scaled slave revolt in America to date. Great leaders such as Dr. Martin Luther King Jr. used religion to unite Black people, stand against racism, and take a peaceful approach to the battle over desegregation. Today religion continues to be a powerful tool for Black people. Churches, such as T.D. Jakes Potter's House, report congregations as large as 30,000 members and are known as mega churches which now shape the community. Leaders continue to use these numbers to bring attention to racial issues and political struggles that African Americans continue to be challenged with. According to a U.S. Religious Landscape Survey conducted in 2007 by the Pew Research Center's Forum on Religion & Public Life:

Black Americans "are markedly more religious on a variety of measures than the U.S. population as a whole." It cited that 87% of Blacks (vs. 83% of all Americans) are affiliated with a religion. It also found that 79% of Blacks (vs. 56% overall) say that religion is "very important in their life." (University of California Berkeley, 2013)

Not only did early African Americans learn the language and adopt Christianity, but they have also used it as a tool to unite Blacks throughout difficult times and times of celebration.

African American men such as William Whipper and William Leidesdorf demonstrated that Blacks could prosper in the United States despite the color of their skin. Several men freed and escaped slavery to find enterprise in the Northern United States. They opened catering businesses, barbershops, laundry services, and worked as what we refer to today as day workers. Amazingly enough, these entrepreneurs pooled their money to better the conditions for other Blacks in their community and helped foster the Underground Railroad, aiding escaped slaves to reach freedom. The will to prosper and earn an honest living in America has led to African Americans not only becoming corporate executives but to start their own multimillion-dollar corporations. Statistics show:

Black owned businesses in the United States increased 60.5% between 2002 and 2007 totaling 1.9 million Black firms. More than 94% of these businesses are made up of sole proprietorships or partnerships which have no paid employees. Nearly 4 in 10 black-owned businesses (more than 700,000) in 2007 operated in the health care, social assistance, and other services, such as repair, maintenance, personal, and laundry services sectors. Administrative Support, waste management, and remediation services made up 11% of Black-owned firms totaling 216,763. Transportation and warehousing was the fourth largest industry making up 9% of Black firms. Despite the 60.5% increase of firms, 55% increase of receipts, and 13% increase of businesses with paid employees, Black-owned businesses only make up 7% of all U.S firms and less than a half percent of all U.S business receipts. African American Adults (ages 10 and up) make up 10% of the adult population and are therefore underrepresented in the U.S. in terms of business ownership especially when it comes to earnings. (U.S. Census Bureau, 2013)

With better education and more opportunities than ever, African Americans are striving to earn fair representation in America's business markets.

My research also found that African American men have served in every major military conflict in the United States and abroad. The first documented act took place at the Boston Massacre. An escaped slave named Crispus Attucks, working as a dock worker in Boston, was leading a mob in protest of the British presence and taxes imposed on the colonies. A nervous British Soldier fired into the crowd, killing Attucks and marking the beginning of the American Revolution. I highlighted the military careers of some profound African American military leaders such the first African American General, Benjamin O. Davis Sr., and the most successful,

Colin Powell, who led forces in Vietnam and the Persian Gulf.

Despite receiving less pay, rations, and substandard care, Black men continued to join the ranks and contribute to the defense of America. Here are the facts:

In 1776, Congress passed legislation that allowed Black men to enlist in the Armed Services. In response to this Congressional Act, approximately 7,000 Black men joined the Army and defended America in the Revolutionary War. In 1948, President Truman signed Executive Order #9981 officially ending segregation in the military. As of FY09, Black Soldiers comprised approximately 20% of the active-duty Army, 13% of the Army National Guard, and 22% of the Army Reserve. Although there are no recruitment goals for racial/ethnic groups, the Army has maintained a force representative of our Nation's diversity, reflecting a belief that all American citizens have equal obligation to provide for the national defense. (Maxfield, 1998) This speaks volumes for a Race of Americans that Whites were afraid to arm.

The last area examined was African American men involved in the U.S. government. I found that Blacks were active in the government from as early as 1834. Alexander Twilight was the first African American elected to a political office. From that date Blacks began to get involved in every level of government from City Alderman to President of the United States. They have had most of their success as Mayors.

The majority of United States politicians have been White, but African Americans have been involved in politics in other ways for centuries. Pioneers such as Fredrick Douglass became ambassadors, advisors, commentators, and voters. The United States Census Bureau reported that two in three eligible blacks (66.2 percent) voted in the 2012 presidential election. This was recorded as the highest voting turnout by

African Americans ever and the first time that Blacks have voted at a higher rate than Whites since the Census Bureau started publishing statistics on voting by the eligible citizen population in 1996 (United States Census Bureau, 2013).

Early politicians, such as Hiram Rhodes Revels, laid the foundation for Barack Obama's historic run for Senate and the Presidency of the United States. Obama became only the fifth African American elected to the United States Congress and the first to hold the Presidential office of the United States.

The takeaway from this project is that some generations of Americans may not realize the sacrifice Blacks made in the making of the United States. An entire race of people was introduced to the country as slaves; that race of people has fought with every resource available to be included in the American Dream. Success can be measured in several ways, one being survival, another could be by the contributions they made, or by simple statistics. African American people still must continue to strive for inclusion and help America continue the dream that all citizens have the right to life, liberty, and the pursuit of happiness. The most interesting fact about this entire project is that in every area I examined White Americans attempted to block, intimidate, and even eliminate Blacks altogether. This proves that African Americans possess a tremendous amount of faith, intelligence, strength, and will power that has delivered them out of slavery and into the here and now.

References

Online Highways LLC. (2013). Nat Turner. Retrieved from U.S. History.com: http://www.u-s-history.com/pages/h3747.html

A+E Networks LLC. (2013). Booker T. Washington Biography- Facts, Birthday, Life Story. Retrieved 1996, from Bio.com: http://www.biography.com/people/booker-t-washington-9524663?page=2

A+E Television Networks, LLC. (2013). Slavery In America. Retrieved 1996, from http://www.history.com: http://www.history.com/topics/slavery

A+E Television Networks, LLC. (2013). Nat Turner Biography-Facts, Birthday, Life Story. Retrieved 1996, from Biography.com: http://www.biography.com/people/nat-turner-9512211

Adscape International, LLC. (2011). The Black Iinventor. Retrieved 1998, from Black Inventor.com: http://www.blackinventor.com/pages/percy-julian.html

Archdiocese of Chicago. (2013). Tolton Canonization. org. Retrieved from Father Augustus Totlon: Cause for Canonization: http://www.toltoncanonization.org/biography/biography_14.html

Bank.WBGH, R. (2013). PBS Online. Retrieved from African In America; The Terrible Transformation: http://www.pbs.org

Bank.WBGH, R. (2013). PBS Online Part 4. Retrieved from African is America;Judgement Day: http://www.pbs.org/wgbh/aia/part4/4h2933.html

Biography.com. (2013). Al Sharpton Biography. Retrieved from Bio.com: http://www.biography.com/people/al-sharpton-207640?page=2

Biography.com. (2013). Frederick Douglass Biography. Retrieved from Bio.com: http://www.biography.com/people/frederick-douglass-9278324?page=3

Biography.com. (2013). George Washington Carver. Retrieved from Biography.com: http://www.biography.com/people/george-washington-carver-9240299

Biography.com. (2013). Jesse Jackson Biography. Retrieved from Bio.com: http://www.biography.com/people/jesse-jackson-9351181?page=2

Biography.com. (2013). Martin Luther King Jr. Biography. Retrieved from Biography.com: http://www.biography.com/people/martin-luther-king-jr-9365086?page=6

Biography.com. (2013). Percy Julian Biography. Retrieved 1996, from Biography.com: http://www.biography.com/people/percy-julian-9359018

Catholic Diocese of Memphis. (2011, Nov). First African Priest. Retrieved from African American Ministry: http://africanamericanministry.com/2011/firstblackpriest

Cozzens, L. (1998). State of Blacks. Retrieved 1995, from Watson.org: http://www.watson.org/~lisa/blackhistory/post-civilwar/reconstruction.html

Darlene Clark Hine, W. H. (n.d.). African Americans: A Concise History (Third Edition). Upper Saddle River, NJ: Pearson Prentice Hall.

First African Baptist Church. (2013). Retrieved from First Africa N B C . com: http://firstafricanbc.com/history.asp

Fremarjo Enterprises, Inc. (2011). A Short Biography of Frederick Douglass . Retrieved 2007, from frederickdouglass.org: http://www.frederickdouglass.org/douglass_bio.html

Gambao, S. (2012). High School Graduation Rate For Black Males Trails White Students. Retrieved from Huffington Post: http://www.huffingtonpost.com/2012/09/19/black-male-hs-graduation-_n_1896490.html

General Secretary. (2013). African Methodist Episcopal

Church. Retrieved from AME Church.com: http://www. ame-church.com/our-church/our-history/

Gleaner Company. (2013, Sept.). discoverjamaica.com. Retrieved from Geography & History of Jamaica: 1783 -1807 Rodney's victory to the abolition of the slave trade: http://www.discoverjamaica.com/history3.htm

Gourley, B. (2013). The American Civil War. Retrieved from Religion and the American Civil War: http://www. brucegourley.com/civilwar/gourleyhistor7.htm#_edn1

Henretta, J. (1997). Early America .Com. Retrieved from Richard Allen: http://www.earlyamerica.com/review/ spring97/allen.html

Henretta, J. (1997, Spring). Richard Allen. Retrieved from Early America. com: http://www.earlyamerica.com/review/ spring97/allen.html

Hynes, G. C. (1974). A Biographical Sketch of W.E.B. DuBois. Retrieved from DuBoisBio.html: http://www.du-boislc.org

Interior, U. D. (n.d.). Slavery and Civil War. Retrieved from National Park Service: www.nps.gov

Islam, N. o. (2010). Wikipedia.com. Retrieved from His-troy of the Nation of Islam: http://en.wikipedia.org/wiki/ Nation_of_Islam

Jenkins, M. C. (2011, 04). Fort Sumter Civil War. Re-trieved from Nation Geographic: http://news.nationalgeo-graphic.com

Klu Klux Klan 1868. (2006). Retrieved from Eye Witness History.com: http://www.eyewitnesstohistory.com/kkk.htm

Library, C. (2013). Early National Education. Retrieved from   Chesapeake: http://www.chesapeake.edu/Library/ EDU_101/eduhist_earlynat.asp

Masons, P. H. (2014). Prince Hall Memorial Education and Scholarship Fund. Retrieved 2011, from http://phmesf. com/

McNamara, R. (n.d.). The Election of 1860 Brings Abraham Lincoln to the White House. Retrieved from 19th Century History: http://history1800s.about.com/od/presidentialcampaigns/a/1860election.htm

Mickens, M. (2006). A Man of Many First : George Liele. Retrieved from Christiantimelines.com : http://www.christiantimelines.com/George%20Liele.htm

Museum of Living History. (2010). A Love Affair With the Brain. Retrieved 1996, from American Academy of Acheivment.org: http://www.achievement.org/autodoc/page/bla1bio-1

NAACP. (2013). NAACP History: W.E.B DuBois. Retrieved from NAACP.ORG: http://www.naacp.org

Nation of Islam. (2013). Nation of Islam.org. Retrieved from Elijah Muhammad: http://noi.org/about_the_honorable_elijah_muhammad.shtml

National Academy of Sciences. (2013). African American History Program. Retrieved 2002, from Keith L. Black: http://www.cpnas.org/aahp/biographies/keith-l-black.html

National Action Network House of Justice. (2013). National Action Network. Retrieved 2011, from nationalactionnetwork.net: http://nationalactionnetwork.net/about/

National Museums Liverpool. (2013). Africa before European slavery. Retrieved from International Slavery Museum (Liverpool).

PBS Online. (2013). Africans In America: Resource Bank Teache'rs Guide. Retrieved from People & Events Prince Hall 1735-1807: http://www.pbs.org/wgbh/aia/part2/2p37.html

PBS Online, W. G. (2013). Slavery and the Making of America. Retrieved from Slavery Experience: Education, Arts, and Color.: http://www.pbs.orgl

Perez, S. (2013). Slavery in the Western Hemisphere: Salve religion. Retrieved from Antebellum Slavery: Plantation

Slave Life: http://cghs.dadeschools.net/slavery/antebellum_
slavery/plantation _slave_life/diet_religion/ religion.htm

Rainbow/PUSH. (2013). Rainbow/ PUSH Coalition.
Retrieved from rainbowpush.org: http://rainbowpush.org/
pages/brief_history

Real people For Real Change. (2003). Al Sharpton's Skle-
ton Closet. Retrieved from realchange.org: http://www.real-
change.org/sharpton.htm

Sanders, N. (2010). America's Black Founders: Revolu-
tionar yHeros and Early Leaders. Chicago, Illinois: Chicago
Review Press.

Schomburg Center. (n.d.). The Abolition of the Slave
Trade. Retrieved from The U.S. Constitution and Acts; Act
of 1807: http://abolition.nypl.org/essays/us_constitution/5/

Slavery and African American Religion. (1997). Retrieved
from Encyclopedia.com: http://www.encyclopedia.com/
doc/1G2-2536600634.html

The King Center. (2013). The King Center. Retrieved
2012, from thekingcenter.org: http://www.thekingcenter.
org/birth-family

The Nobel Foundation 1964. (2013, Aug 2). Nobel Prizes
and Laureates; Martin Luther King Jr. - Biographical. Retrieved from Nobel Prize.org: http://www.nobelprize.org /
nobel _prizes/peace/laureates/1964/king-bio.html

University, A. (2011, Nov 28). Life in the 18th Century/
Advances in Education in the 1700s. Retrieved from Library
Guides.com: http://andersonuniversity.libguides.com /con-
tent. php?pid=267041&sid=2289982

Walsh, R. (1829). Aboard a Slave Ship. Retrieved 2000,
from EyeWitness to History: www.eyewitnesstohistory.com

Washington, A. (2012). U.S. black male graduation rates
lag behind whites. Retrieved from USA Today: http://us-
atoday30.usatoday.com/news/nation/story/2012/09/19/us-
black-male-graduation-rates-lag/57807392/1

WGBH. (2013). African in America Part II / Salvery and Religion. Retrieved from PBS Online: http://www.pbs.org/wgbh/aia/part2/2narr2.html

Williams, A. H. (2004). Self Taught: African American education in slavery and freedom. Chapel Hill : University of North Carolina Press.

ABOUT THE AUTHOR

CHARLES LUCAS was born in 1969 in the small farming community of Lake Village, Arkansas. He joined the military after graduating high school and has had multiple deployments involving peace keeping missions, combat tours, natural disaster relief, large scale training events, and he continues to serve today. He settled in Little Rock, Arkansas in 1995 where he started a family and had one son. Charles continued to work on his education while maintaining full time employment. Truly a shovel to a desk type of story. His father taught him to "work for the things you want and believe in yourself." This book is important to him because it is about what others have been through which enabled us to achieve the things we all have: Life, Liberty, and the Pursuit of Happiness. Charles says, "I felt there needed to a be source of credible information about the greatness of African America men and paint a picture of the struggles of the past that still are present in different forms today. I noticed that very little time is spent on the achievements of African American men. Our sons and daughters need a short, comprehensible walk through the past that may be shared with peers of all races so that they will know what it took to get us to the here and now. Thank You and Enjoy!"

Also Available from J. Kenkade Publishing

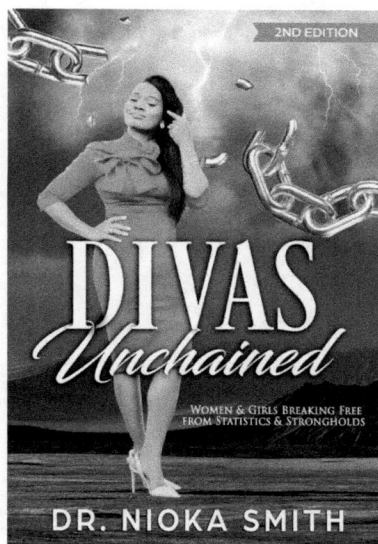

ISBN: 978-1-944486-25-9
Visit www.drniokasmith.com
Author: Dr. Nioka Smith

Sexually abused by her father at the age of 14, pregnant at the age of 17, and a nervous breakdown at the age of 28, Dr. Nioka Smith's painful past almost killed her, until the voice of the Lord guided her into destroying strongholds and reversing Satan's plan for her life. DIVAS Unchained is the powerful chain-breaking reality of the many unfortunate strongholds our women and girls face. Dr. Nioka uses her divine gift to help women and girls break free from destructive life cycles and prosper in all areas of life. Satan has lied to you. It's time to expose his lies. It's time to break free!

Also Available from
J. Kenkade Publishing

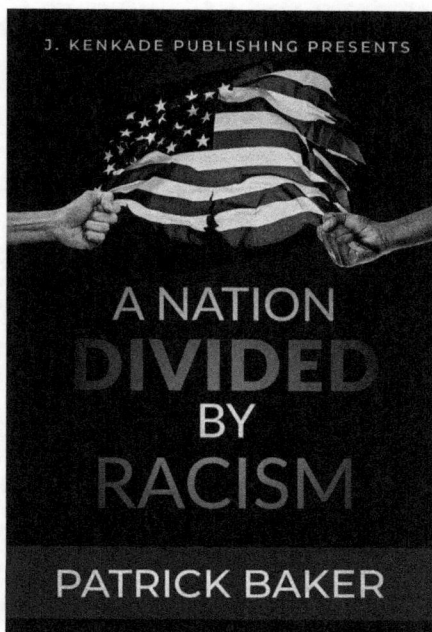

ISBN: 978-1-944486-54-9

Purchase at www.amazon.com

Author: Patrick Baker

We live in a world where, although we share the world with different people and ethnicities, we live with hate, malice, envy, and strife toward one another. "A Nation Divided by Racism" addresses these matters within an open dialogue.

Also Available from
J. Kenkade Publishing

J. KENKADE PUBLISHING PRESENTS

THE *Face* OF
THE *New*
ENGINEER

Dr. Lashun K. Massey

ISBN: 978-1-944486-53-2
Purchase at www.amazon.com
Author: Dr. Lashun K. Massey

This book provides an account of the life story of Dr. Lashun King Massey, P.E. It outlines the challenges that she faced growing up as a child in rural Arkansas. Although Dr. Massey was born in a socioeconomically depressed area in Arkansas, she managed to defy the odds and pursue a career in engineering. This book helps to tell the story of Dr. Massey's childhood life and uncover the challenges that she faced in pursuing a career in engineering.

Also Available from
J. Kenkade Publishing

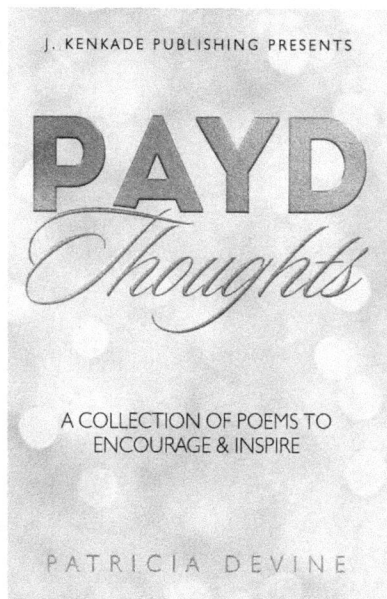

J. KENKADE PUBLISHING PRESENTS

PAYD
Thoughts

A COLLECTION OF POEMS TO
ENCOURAGE & INSPIRE

PATRICIA DEVINE

ISBN: 978-1-944486-64-8

Purchase at www.amazon.com

Author: Patricia Devine

"PAYD Thoughts" is a collection of poems that focus on various subjects inspired by the author's experiences shared with the hope of encouraging and inspiring readers in similar situations. "PAYD Thoughts" discusses race relations, love towards God, unhealthy relationships, depression and more.

This page intentionally left blank
by J. Kenkade Publishing

www.ingramcontent.com/pod-product-compliance
Lightning Source LLC
LaVergne TN
LVHW051130080426
835510LV00018B/2336